The Unsigned, Undelivered Letter

The Unsigned, Undelivered Letter

Pindling Left Free . . . Mandela Set Free

Philip Rahming

CONTENTS

To

Her Excellency Dame Marguerite Pindling
Governor General, The Commonwealth of The Bahamas

The Hon. Dr. Hubert Minnis
Prime Minister, The Commonwealth of The Bahamas

His Excellency Cyril Ramaphosa President,
The Republic of South Africa

My parents, Lennie and Rebecca (both deceased)
My twin siblings, Isadora and Lenora (deceased)
My daughter Philippa, My granddaughter Aaliyah,
Rehoboth Ministries, Prince Charles Drive, Nassau, The Bahamas

ACKNOWLEDGMENTS

I AM INDEBTED TO Joan Rolle, curriculum specialist, for her assistance in drafting *The Unsigned, Undelivered Letter*, Samira Azzahir for her editing services; former Governor General of the Bahamas Dame Marguerite Pindling for her permission to use a selection of speeches by Sir Lynden Pindling; Eddie Minnis and Stan Burnside for permission to include cartoons from *The Potluck* and *Sideburns*, respectively; Elliene Carron, editor of the *Tribune* for permission to use the front page of the *Tribune* dated April 28, 1977; and former senator Dr. Jacinta Higgs and Pastor Dr. James Shearer, BDiv, JP for consenting to draft the forewords to *The Unsigned, Undelivered Letter*.

I am also indebted to Rev. Dr. Arthur Roach for his contribution to the chapter on Sir Lynden. Finally, I say thank you to Alexa-Rae Smith my grandniece for her assistance, Terry Johnson for the front cover design and my niece Wendy Cartwright for the back-page design. Your additions to this book are invaluable and much appreciated.

It is my most humble and singular gratitude to write the foreword for such an epic story. Rev. Dr. Philip Rahming is blessed to be able to share this wealth of history with the people of the Bahamas. This book is a powerful teaching to see how far-reaching our influence can be, regardless of size or circumstance. Bahamians can change the world. Bahamians can change the course of history. I salute Rev. Dr. Philip Rahming for his decision to share the story behind the undelivered letter.

FOREWORD

IHAVE KNOWN DR. Philip A. Rahming all my life. I remember him from the radio, I heard his sermons on Sundays, I read about his work and struggles in the newspaper, and I celebrated his position as a lecturer at the College of the Bahamas, now the University of the Bahamas. His continued love for the community of Fox Hill and his fierce pride in being Bahamian have been a source of inspiration for me as I pursued and accomplished one academic degree after the next. As a senator, every time I recited the national pledge, I became increasingly thankful for Dr. Rahming, who wrote it. I proudly followed his exemplary leadership, and now I embrace the honor of his presence as a presenter for my Akhepran staff and scholars, as my role of principal and educator in my own beloved Fox Hill.

As I look back on my life as another child of Fox Hill village, I recognize the value and importance of knowledge of self. As Bahamians, we are rich with history: we have direct ties to our ancestral languages and places of origin; we have kept a close and detailed account of our community and its happenings; we have stood up and claimed our country and our right to govern ourselves with intelligence and integrity.

I take so much pride in seeing what we have accomplished in such a short time. Yet I also see a growing need to pass this knowledge on to our younger generations of Bahamians. We sit here in beauty and abundance—

our country lies in some of the most coveted waters on Earth. Our lands are visited by people from all over the world. We have so much to be thankful for. The question is, how do we move forward? This book is an awesome step in the right direction, and again, I salute Rev. Dr. Philip Rahming for writing this book.

Dr. Jacinta M. Higgs Ed.D
Akhepran International Academy

ABOUT THE AUTHOR

HE IS A wonderful man, an eminent longtime servant of the Lord. He understands best his role in human history and God's sovereignty.

The name Dr. Philip Arthur Rahming is one of the brightest stars to shine in the Fox Hill community. He is well known and loved. He loves serving the Commonwealth of the Bahamas in every facet of his life, especially as a pastor.

He spent most of his years in the educational construction of the Bahamas and higher studies abroad. After which he retired from the College of the Bahamas, the highest academic institute in the country, as a social scientist. He is my friend.

Dr. Philip Arthur Rahming understands absolutely that change is truly an inevitable factor on the road to human development. His faith and works are portrayed meticulously in the purity of Bahamian politics. The presentation of his governmental concepts reveals a microscopic and telescopic comprehension of the Christian worldview.

The author is generally a winner in most of his life's endeavors.

Pastor Dr. James Shearer, BDiv, JP

PREFACE

IN THE DYING months of my seventy-eighth birthday in the year 2011, something clicked within me. I was remembering a historic undelivered letter and the private and painful burden I bore for a time to keep this letter undelivered. My reflections took me back to the 1985 Commonwealth Heads of Government Meeting (CHOGM) held in Nassau, Bahamas. The Commission of Inquiry into whether or not the first prime minister, Sir Lynden Pindling, had any involvement in drug trafficking proceeds, was over in late 1983, and its outcome was almost and probably forgotten by the general population.

The commission concluded that there was no credible evidence directly linking Sir Lynden to drug-related charges and corruption. Pindling's exoneration occurred three months before the surfacing of this letter, which was drafted by some members of the Bahamas Christian Council. I heard about the letter prior to it being brought to the council for discussion, and at the time, it was agreed that the president of the council should sign and deliver the letter to the prime minister. It appeared to me that the council was placing itself in a position to do what the Commission of Inquiry did not. It seemed to be the hope of many that the commission would have removed Sir Lynden Pindling from power.

As president of the Bahamas Christian Council, I did not authorize the drafting of this letter. I did not sign it, nor did I deliver it. The whole affair was a public and private struggle for me, but I firmly stood my ground and did not allow the letter to reach its intended destination through any orchestrating on my part. There was a force or spirit within me all along that was leading me in another direction. When it was all over, I mentioned my dilemma to Sir Lynden and found out, to my surprise, that he himself was quite aware of the existence of the letter. He said that he was only waiting for me to make my move, and then he would make his.

The CHOGM got under way in October 1985, and as the host nation, our prime minister Sir Lynden was its chairman. On the agenda was the problematic apartheid regime in South Africa coupled with the urgent need to *release* Nelson Mandela from prison. Sensitive meetings were held on the weekend of CHOGM at Lyford Cay. A special committee met and finally came up with a plan to bring an end to the apartheid system in South Africa and have Nelson Mandela released.

I did not deliver the letter and because of this, it is my belief that Prime Minister Pindling was left free to perform his duties as host of CHOGM. Delivering the letter could have hindered our prime minister in the execution of his duties, to be and appear at his best in his role as host of the historic CHOGM. Delivering the letter could have seriously jeopardized this.

I likened my role in this endeavor to a mouse helping the lion and setting it free. The mouse chewed the rope that had ensnared the lion, and the lion was able to muscle itself out into freedom. If I may take this analogy one step further, I will venture to liken Sir Lynden to the mouse and South Africa to the lion and out of the lion came the giant Mandela, whom the world seemingly was awaiting, a world that was yearning for his kind of leadership, one based on reconciliation.

I would venture to declare that the first prime minister of the Bahamas, Sir Lynden Oscar Pindling, perhaps accomplished his greatest foreign policy goal, all because this letter remained undelivered. A letter delivered may not have allowed for such a great feat to occur.

I give God thanks for the courage and guidance all along the way. He allowed me to keep this letter in my possession until now, when its sting has been lost and its victory taken away. As we become older as a sovereign nation and produce outstanding citizens, we Bahamians need to know of events such as this one. This kind of knowledge would serve as an inspiration to our up- and-coming young people, encouraging them to take action and stand for the greater good and the advancement of mankind here at home and anywhere in the world. This is of particular importance as we stand now, looking onward to the next generation of independent Bahamians as we continue to ask God to bless our sunny clime.

If the lion does not tell its story, then the hunter will tell its tail.

*This anthem, our National Song and first runner-up to the Bahamas National Anthem, was sung on October 14, 1985, in the presence of Her Majesty Queen Elizabeth II and some twenty-five thousand persons at Clifford Park. It was sung in 2012 for her grandson, Prince Harry, by school children for a capacity crowd at the new Thomas A. Robinson Stadium.

CHAPTER 1

The Letter

IN A DRAWER of my desk in the study, locked away beneath some old notebooks, there is a letter addressed to the Father of Our Nation from a governing body that is still one of the most influential organizations in the country today. Sir Lynden Oscar Pindling, however, never read this letter; and I, the two-time president of the Bahamas Christian Council (BCC), never delivered it. I was asked to deliver this letter by fellow members of the Bahamas Christian Council during my second term as its president, at a time when our nation's first prime minister would be involved in one the most important foreign policy negotiations of his career.

Sir Lynden was never one to take a personal affront lightly. He had a reputation for cutting down adversaries, marginalizing opponents, and circumventing opposition. These factors had to be considered when anyone contemplated approaching Sir Lynden. They were certainly near the top of my list as I reflected on the wisdom and prudence of approaching him with a document that I had no part in crafting or authorizing as president of the Christian Council. Surprisingly, Sir Lynden revealed to me in the years after information about the letter that it was circulated and discussed in the community and that he knew of its existence; he was just waiting for me to make my move, and then he would make his. And how did Sir Lynden find out about the existence of the letter even before its delivery? It is my belief that certain members of the BCC engaged in a preemptive strike seeking to distance themselves from the letter and placing it squarely upon my shoulders at its delivery. Some may ask, "So what was the big deal about the letter? What effect could it have had on the actions of Sir Lynden? All he had to do was to sweep it under the rug after its delivery, but the letter, even in its undelivered state, was already in the radar of the press.

The contents of the letter were, in my opinion, indeed shocking, judgmental, and condemnatory. The council addressed the prime minister as though he were a *rogue schoolboy*. I felt disappointed by the contents of the letter, and the request to deliver it presented itself as a sudden and heavy load on my shoulders. I also felt an uncharacteristic level of fear come over me as I thought about the outcomes of both delivering the letter and not delivering it. It was the classic situation of "damned if I do and damned if I don't." This is the position I found myself in as president of the Bahamas Christian Council. I saw no way out.

There was a special call meeting of the BCC to discuss the letter and its delivery. As we were leaving that historic meeting, which I now call Letter Day, a member of the council, a close friend of Sir Lynden, came to me and requested that after signing the letter, I should make a copy of it for him. This was a very unusual request coming from him, and it made me begin to think that there was more to this situation than meets the eye. Did this letter and the circumstances surrounding its drafting go deeper?

I said to myself, *What is this? What is happening? What is going on that I am not privy to?* I did not know how to respond as I walked away from my associate.

The members of the council believed that I would easily agree to deliver the letter. They did not expect me to do otherwise. Looking back on those years, I feel that, had it been my first three-year term as president of the council, I would have capitulated and readily delivered the letter, but it was my second term in office, and I had become seasoned in the role. In my first term as president, inexperience would have driven me to perform the act, and I would have considered myself as being guided rightly by the collective mind. In retrospect, I came to understand that my first term was to learn what was required and the second term was to do what was required.

On that fateful day, I did not go straight home but went instead to the church of the treasurer of the council, Pastor Richard Sands, whom I felt might assist me in my understanding the motives behind the drafting of the letter, its tone, and its contents. He offered me no details no matter how intensely I questioned him. Perhaps he himself knew nothing. So I took another approach and asked him what he would do if he were the president. He said in reply, "Well, brother, since all the big boys say deliver it, I would deliver it." I got the impression that he meant exactly what he said. Ironically, what I got from the brother was a little bit of soberness, courage, and strength to hold off on delivering the letter. I needed to reflect upon my impending actions until I could fully comply with what I was being asked to do. I wanted to proceed with an understanding and conviction I could live with, as this would be necessary to defend the contents of the letter because, after all, I was to deliver it to the leader of our nation.

A week had passed. During this time, whenever I ran into members of the council, they would inquire as to whether I had delivered the letter. My response was always, "No, not yet." The longer I took to make the delivery, the more strongly I felt to delay the process. I finally had a private meeting with a fellow clergyman, Archdeacon Murillo Bonaby, who was not a member of the council, to seek some advice. I asked, "What must I do?"

His response was "Lead!"

I looked him in the eye and asked, "What do you mean by lead?"

He said a second time, "Lead!" At this point, I remembered President J. F. Kennedy saying that all a leader needed was the ability to lead and to lead vigorously.

Lead? How strange. Everything around me seemed to be quiet and still. No one came by and said, "I have your back" or "We have your back." The mood around me seemed to be "He delivered that letter yet? What is he waiting for?" Meanwhile, as I stated previously, the prime minister knew of the existence of the letter. We would attend annual church conventions to bring greetings from the government and from the Bahamas Christian Council. We kept meeting and speaking with each other. I suppose that even the prime minister was watching to see how and when I would deliver the letter, but you know what? I did not see the seriousness of the matter or its consequences then as I can see it now, and thank God for that. I believe that if I had known the true nature of the situation, it would have been too much stress, too much pain for me to carry.

Members of the Christian Council and some members of the press were waiting for the ball to drop out of my hand. All I can say is God and God alone sustained me. Now, looking back, I do not see how I got out of the situation except by the grace of God. It is my belief that God took the painful responsibility away from me. He had bigger plans for us all. I say this because the letter situation presented itself right at the time when the heads of government of commonwealth nations and its monarch, Queen Elizabeth II, would be in the Bahamas. As far as I could ascertain, however, our internal struggles remained unknown to the international audience who attended the meeting. I asked myself, *Is this a reflection of the quality of Bahamians?* We would fuss and fight among ourselves, but when the stranger comes in, we close ranks, and they never know of the turmoil within. Suffice it to say that all I know is that the Commonwealth Heads of Government Meeting (CHOGM) proceeded as planned, and the letter remained undelivered.

Let me now mention a dream told by the late Uchal Johnson of Mission Baptist Church on Hay Street. I recently contacted his wife, Mrs. Nazel Johnson, to check on the details of the dream. She does not remember him relaying the dream to her. This was approximately thirty-three years ago, but here is the dream as he told it to me:

> It was on a Sunday after the 11:00 a.m. Divine Worship Service. He said that he left his church in a rush to meet me at my church, Mt. Carey Union Baptist Church in Fox Hill. When he came, only the pastor, Rev. Leopold D. Cox and Rev. Randolph Armbrister and I were there putting things in place before we left. Uchal came filled with excitement. He said that he had a dream last night. In this dream, the prime minister wanted to leave his office to go to the House of Parliament, but the crowd refused to let him go to parliament. There was a great commotion, and then one person said, "Send for Philip Rahming." More and more voices joined in and said, "Send for Philip Rahming." Before they could send for me, he said he woke up.

When this young Baptist layman told me his dream with passion, I felt a little embarrassed and uneasy because there I was with my pastor and his assistant being regarded with so much importance in that dream.

Uchal seemed a little disappointed that I did not respond with much interest, but even though I felt an inner excitement, I had to tone it down in the presence of my seniors; and as a matter of fact, I later cast it out of my mind. Over the years, I forgot about it until I began to feel the urge to write this book. My problem here with this dream is that Uchal, Reverend Cox, and Reverend Armbrister have all gone on in death, and his wife does not recall being told the dream, so I am now the only one with the memory.

My interpretation of the dream, upon reflection, was that I was being called and singled out to deliver the prime minister from whatever the situation was and to set him free to move into areas where his leadership was needed on an international level as the question of sanctions against South Africa and the freeing of Nelson Mandela was brewing.

I hope that when this book is published, however, someone who still remembers hearing of this dream will come forward. I believe that it was good that I had forgotten the dream over these past years because it may have, in some way, influenced me to act without counting the cost in the drama of this unsigned and undelivered letter.

After being advised to lead, I did not seek advice from any other person but turned instead to the greatest source of all advice—God. As I turned the situation over in my mind, I asked God to lead me and to keep me strong in my convictions. This was not a simple matter. It was one that had national, if not international, consequences as well. It could serve to add fuel to an already-raging fire, at the heart of which was our national leader, Sir Lynden Pindling. Was our nation, our government, and even our leader intimately involved with notorious drug traffickers such as Carlos Joe Leeder? Did he have a part in causing our Bahamaland to be dubbed "a nation for sale"? The cries of "LO, LO, LO, gat to go" and "the chief is a thief" were echoing throughout the nation.

During this time, another situation was unfolding on the world scene in the Philippines, where, after fifteen consecutive years as supreme ruler, the leadership of Ferdinand Marcos was being challenged. The leadership of Sir Lynden was being compared to that of Marcos—if not in style and philosophy, then in longevity. His wife, Lady Marguerite, was being compared to Imelda Marcos in her sense of fashion. This added fuel to the opposition's fire: "the chief is a thief" and "LO, LO, LO, gat to go!"

It was during this time, while driving home, that I happened to pass by a Free National Movement rally that was being held on R. M. Bailey Park. You can only imagine my shock when I heard a speaker at the podium shouting, "Philip Rahming, Philip Rahming has to go!" This, I assumed, may have been in response to my holding on to the letter. It had now become public knowledge and was up for political debate. It was then, for the first time, that I felt the true weight and gravity of the situation I was in.

The matter of the letter found its way into the press and onto the airwaves. The cruelest cut of all, however, was the proclamation at that political rally: "Philip Rahming has got to go," and the crowd cheered. That night, I went home and, sprawling out on the kitchen floor facedown before God, asked him to keep me strong and to protect and lead me. I was becoming afraid, and rightfully so; for at one point, it was found that someone had deliberately placed gunpowder in the engine of my car. One sputter and it could have gone up in flames. The weight of public opinion was on my shoulders, and still, I had no pressing desire to deliver the letter, no compelling urge to follow through. I had not had a pastorate since returning from Southern Baptist Theological Seminary in 1971, and during this time, I took up a lectureship at the Bahamas Teacher's College, which later became the College of the Bahamas, now the University of the Bahamas. Now and then, as I would pass students on my way to class, some would say, "Sign the letter! Deliver the letter!" I did notice, however, that none of the students I taught directly ever brought up the matter of the letter in class.

Criticism and condemnation were coming from many quarters. I recall being contacted by one of the daily newspapers and being asked the most popular question of the day: "Do you have any comments to make on the letter?"

My response at that time was "Silence is golden." As they reported on my response, this statement took center stage in the minds and pens of the journalists. To further place the letter within the context of the day, one must keep in mind that the findings of the Commission of Inquiry into drug trafficking in the Bahamas had just been made public in December 1984, just three months prior to the drafting of the letter. The findings of the commission stated that the drug trade had saturated the Bahamian society. It went on further to say that even though Sir Lynden was not directly involved in the trade, he had spent eight times more money than he had earned in a seven- year period.[1]

The Commission of Inquiry was established by Sir Lynden himself to investigate allegations made by the press in the United States, for example, the *Miami Herald* and NBC television station, concerning his personal involvement and the Bahamian government's involvement in the drug trade. According to a *Nassau Guardian* report dated March 27, 1984, Brian Ross had identified Mr. Robert Vesco a few months prior as a drug smuggler who resided in the Bahamas, where he carried on a major drug trafficking operation with the cooperation of the Bahamian government led by Sir Lynden. It was alleged that Vesco was paying $100,000 per month for this protection. We were being dubbed as "a nation for sale."

Amid these serious allegations, the letter delivered may have driven the final nail into the life of our newly evolving sovereign nation led by one of the sons of the nation. It may have even ended the political career of this son who, after all, had led the Bahamas in the Quiet Revolution. In fact, we may, in my opinion, have even run the risk of losing our sovereignty. We could have become a nation of Bahamians not being led by Bahamians.

My refusal to deliver the letter caused folks to opine that I would be ousted from the council and another president elected who would be unafraid to carry out the task. The council election of officers was not far away, and the closer they got, the more frequent the threats. Still, I did not become anxious or afraid, nor did I harbor any feelings of guilt or regret. It had to be a power beyond me that caused me not to deliver the letter and, at the same time, to keep my mind and spirit at ease and at peace within the turmoil and struggles that presented themselves. Was I being led and guided by a higher power in my decision not to deliver the letter? Was it the case that the matter was not really in my hands at all and that it was truly under the auspices of a higher power that was saying, "Let the letter remain Undelivered."

I am not an arrogant person. Under normal circumstances, I could have been reminded formally or pressured informally to deliver the letter, and this I might have considered. However, up until now, I was not complying. A higher power was the true captain of the ship. I lived and functioned as normal under the pressure of the circumstance.

---

1   Taken from the letter dated March 18, 1985, from the Bahamas Christian Council to Sir Lynden.

Now to facilitate the delivery of the letter, members of the council commissioned the secretary, Canon Kirkley Sands, to make an appointment with Sir Lynden to discuss the contents of the letter. After the appointment was made, Sands contacted me and requested that I accompany him to the meeting in my capacity as president. Surprised at the turn of events, I quickly refused Sands and told him that I would not be party to any such meeting.

He expressed his disappointment and implored me to attend. I relented and thought it wise to go to keep control of the letter and the situation and therefore agreed to attend the meeting. The men in the council, who I suppose were backing Sands, were men who held responsible positions in their respective churches, so this was not a light matter that I found myself faced with. I believed that if I did not attend the meeting between Reverend Sands and Sir Lynden, it would have left me at a terrible disadvantage that may have haunted me for the rest of my life.

I felt that I had to be there to maintain control not only of my role as president of the Christian Council but also of a situation that could have affected the direction of the country for ill in the final analysis. I also decided to accompany Sands on his quest to deliver the letter because of the clout that the church leaders whom I imagined were backing him had. Their leadership was historic and strong. It was my fear that they may have gotten together in a special meeting and demanded that the letter be delivered.

This move that they had set in motion with Sands at the helm could have spelt the beginning of the end for me. In my opinion, it could have been disastrous. I accompanied Sands to keep a continuous flow in the dialogue and keep control over the destination of this letter. At this point, I began to wonder: Could this have been how the crafting of the letter got under way? Did its creation involve the cooperation and amalgamation of like minds? Was it born within a cell within the BCC, whose existence I was not aware of?

In true form, Sir Lynden greeted us as the statesman he always was. He looked toward me as the president with a questioning expression on his face. I told Sir Lynden that I did not authorize the visit but was only attending in my capacity as president of the BCC to ensure that matters did not get out of hand. Sir Lynden said that he was glad I had chosen to come along because he did not know Father Sands from the council. At that juncture, I called for an end to the meeting, and we left with the letter remaining undelivered.

Another influential church leader, Rev. Charles Saunders, in his role as the president of the Bahamas National Baptist Missionary and Education Convention, was also asked to implore me to deliver the letter (this is what was made known by him to the public in one of the local daily papers at the time). Reverend Saunders refused to try to direct me to deliver the letter. His response was that since I became president of the council, the Baptists had to release me to become a free moral agent.

Meanwhile, the council continued to hold its monthly meetings as we moved steadily into our annual general elections. The opposition against me to remain as president was weak, so once again, I ran for the presidency and was elected, while Father Sands was not returned to office. The election results were strange indeed, as the prevailing sentiment at the time was that they would get rid of Rahming and elect a man who would do as he was told and deliver the letter.

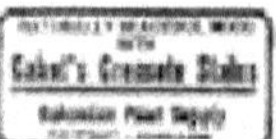

First Term, 1977–1980

Second Term, 1983–1986

So I have outlined some of the history behind the letter and some of the reasons why it was not delivered. I will expand on these reasons in subsequent chapters. What I can now say is that the letter was never delivered, and the passage of time washed away the pain and the need to deliver the letter. To this day, it still remains unsigned and, of course, undelivered.

When events had cooled down surrounding the letter, I visited Sir Lynden and told him of the letter. Without hesitation, Sir Lynden revealed to me that he knew of the existence of the letter; and as stated previously, he was just waiting for me to make my move. and then he would make his. At these words, tears gushed from my eyes, and I informed Sir Lynden that they were not tears of weakness but tears of relief, which came from knowing that I made the right decision at the time.

I had refused to be pushed into a situation that I did not fully understand nor support and did not take into account my opinion.

Sir Lynden never said whether or not he was pleased that the letter was not delivered. He did ask, however, what I would like for him to do for me. I looked at him and he said, "Yes, I am in the chair."

Then I answered him, "If the Lord tells you to give me something, give it." But let me say here that I expected nothing and received nothing. I was concerned about the continued leadership of our country by our own people.

CHAPTER 2

Other Letters

T HERE WERE MANY reasons why I never gave the letter to Sir Lynden, but the reason that sat most heavily on my mind was the fact that it contained information that I had no knowledge of, the chief among these being allegations that Sir Lynden had, according to the letter, accepted "gifts from sources known and unknown."[2] This alleged practice was referred to in the letter as being "morally questionable."

What the drafters of the letter may or may not have been aware of was that Sir Lynden, in November 1984 (four months prior to the drafting of the letter), had sought to explain, in light of allegations that were surfacing in the Commission of Inquiry and foreign newspapers, specifically the *Miami Herald*, one of these "gifts from sources known and unknown." On November 19, 1984, one month before the findings of the Commission of Inquiry were made public, Sir Lynden wrote to me and made available for my scrutiny, copies of correspondences between him, Edward St. George, and D. C. de la Rue, VP of the Grand Bahama Port Authority. The first letter dated October 9, 1978, concerned the construction of a

---

2   Taken from the letter dated March 18, 1985, from the Bahamas Christian
     Council to Sir Lynden.

small hotel in Sir Lynden's constituency. However, the construction of the small hotel/fishing club was abandoned by Mr. St. George, and it was decided to build six houses instead. In his cover letter to me, Sir Lynden revealed that his financial dealings with Mr. St. George, which may be open to adverse commentary, centered around Mr. St. George's desire to assist in the economic growth and development of his constituency in Andros. This was to be achieved by Mr. St. George facilitating the construction of a small hotel. According to Sir Lynden, the project to construct the small hotel came into being in October 1978. In an October 9, 1978, letter written to Mr. St. George, Sir Lynden thanked him for his preliminary work on the project, which included sending a team into the area to conduct an assessment. In the letter, Sir Lynden recommends a possible site and size for the hotel.

In his letter to me, Sir Lynden revealed that particular project was canceled and replaced by an idea to build six rental houses instead. This was communicated to Sir Lynden by Mr. St. George in a letter dated June 11, 1981. In it, Mr. St. George announces the cancelation of the initial project and his desire instead to build six houses in the constituency that could become rental units. A check for $300,000 payable to the Family Island Development Board was enclosed with the letter. Mr. St. George also suggested that the project be done by a particular contractor. According to Sir Lynden, this new project too, however, was canceled ten months after an initial down payment was made to the contractor in July 1981. The full amount of $300,000 was to facilitate various phases of construction including the cost of building materials and creation of an access road. In his letter, Sir Lynden states that by May 1982, not one aspect of the project was started or completed. Therefore, the project was canceled.

In canceling the project to build the houses, Mr. St. George said in a letter to the prime minister dated May 3, 1982, that the funds from the failed project may be used to finance his election campaign and that of Shadrach Morris or any other candidate.

Sir Lynden responded on the twentieth of August 1982, thanking Mr. St. George for permission to use the leftover funds from the failed project. Sir Lynden states that these funds were used to assist both him and Shadrach Morris in their individual campaigns. Further to the canceled project, Sir Lynden stated that he endeavored to seek the return of the funds paid to the contractor but was unsuccessful.

Sir Lynden received an answer to this letter from the vice president and treasurer of the Grand Bahama Port Authority, Limited. In this letter, it was reported that Mr. St. George had no interest in recovering the funds from the contractor, but if Sir Lynden met with success, he was free to use what was recovered.

What the public at large is becoming more and more aware of is the fact that high-ranking officials may have their reputation and legacy tarnished by those whom they put their trust in and whom they surround themselves with. Sir Lynden may have found himself in this position.

As far as I was concerned, this information, proffered by Sir Lynden, was sufficient to explain that particular "gift from sources known and unknown,"[3] to which the drafters of the letter may have been making reference.

---

3   Ibid.

CHAPTER 3

Sir Lynden Oscar Pindling

HAVING BEEN REASSURED by Sir Lynden's explanation of one of the "gifts from sources known and unknown," I now turned to what I knew of the man. This knowledge also helped me to hold off on delivering the letter.

My first encounter with Sir Lynden came in 1961, when I was accepted at Calabar Theological College in Jamaica. At this time, Sir Lynden was already an active presence in Bahamian politics and had a professional office on Shirley Street. I informed Sir Lynden that I was entering Calabar, and he generously donated five pounds to this endeavor. Both of us had something in common—we were concerned about the advancement of our people. We both knew that we needed to affect a change in society that would pull up black Bahamians to a position where we would become equal among men.

My entering Calabar placed me in league with men such as Charles Smith, the former Pastor of Zion Baptist Church, and Bishop Michael Symonette, the general superintendent of St. John's Particular Church of Native Baptist Society. We were young, maturing Baptist ministers striving for educational advancement so that we could aid in the uplifting of our people.

Sir Lynden was a new presence and voice in the community. Very early on in his political career, he recognized the voting power and inf luence of the Baptist Church and sought to establish a relationship with its leaders. Rev. Dr. R. E. Cooper Sr., who was, at one time, aligned with the United Bahamian Party and supported Bobby Symonette in Exuma, now became a great supporter of Sir Lynden and inf luenced other Baptists to do the same.

The community recognized that in the political arena, if you had the Baptists behind you, you had the majority. Around the time of "majority rule," not all denominations supported the Progressive Liberal Party (PLP). Denominations such as the Anglicans, Catholics, and Presbyterians were not seemingly vocal in their support of the Progressive Liberal Party.

I believe that one of the greatest milestones in the life of Sir Lynden was the part that he played in ushering in majority rule in the Bahamas. Sir Lynden showed the people a vision from the mountaintop. He showed them that it was possible to stand upright shoulder to shoulder with the master. He showed them the meaning of people power.

I believe the people were surprised by their own power. It was like the story of the slave who, becoming tired of being beaten by the master, turned on him and beat him to death. As the master lay dead at his feet, the slave said, "Get up, Massa . . . You dead? I didn't know you could die too." He also was surprised by his power.

Over the years, Sir Lynden had become synonymous with the PLP. Some mistakenly consider him the founder of the PLP, but he was not. Three white Bahamians from Long Island, Sir Milton Taylor, Cyril Stevenson, and William Cartwright founded the PLP. They founded this party as a political counterforce to the oligarchy of the day. It is believed that they felt the governing body was ostracizing them, and so the three founders of the PLP formed the party as a means to shake that body up. They only wanted to go so far with the new party, in order to maintain and coexist with those in power, but Sir Lynden wanted to go all the way. In fact, this is how the slogan "PLP, All the Way" came about. Sir Lynden wanted to take us there. Sir Henry and company brought Sir Lynden in to give legal advice, but instead, he took the bull by the horns and took the PLP and the country, "All the Way" to majority rule and independence. It is said that in response to this political avalanche, Sir Henry was heard to have said he "cursed the day when he created that monster," referring to the PLP. Sir Henry Milton was later appointed to the position of governor-general of an independent Bahamas.

Sir Lynden was a master at galvanizing the people, and there was no hypocrisy in him. He was a people person and walked comfortably with kings and commoners alike. I believe Sir Lynden's downfall came from those with whom he worked, loved, and felt most comfortable with. These were the ones, starting with the Dissident Eight, who hoped to be just as great as Sir Lynden. They wanted a piece of the pie in equal leadership. It would seem as if they did this for their own personal reasons, starting with Sir Cecil, who made it clear that he wanted to be a leader.

Sir Lynden was an all-embracing leader who gave opportunities to as many as possible. Sir Lynden would cut you down but do so with compassion and gentleness.

He was very decisive and had no difficulty in letting you know who was in charge. Sir Lynden remained the same visionary, the same compassionate leader that he was in his early days even though the challenges and difficulties were not the same as in the beginning.

The 1980s, for example, was a troubling time for the nation, and the people were warned by Sir Lynden to be on the alert for the fallout. Unfortunately, it would seem that many persons who can be referred to as "influence peddlers" used his name to *ill purpose*. When Sir Lynden was interviewed on the Brian Ross show in the mid '80s, he entered from a position of strength, knowing that he was innocent, but he was playing on the NBC's playing field and was thrown many curve balls that he could not hit. He lost his cool time and time again during the course of the show. He should have kept his cool. Before the taping of the show, I went to Sir Lynden to offer moral support, and I suggested to him that it may be best to listen more than to speak (not that he was obliged to take my suggestion, nor did he ask for any). Years later, I had the opportunity to view President Obama as he was verbally attacked by a white US governor. He countered this aggressive approach with the cool of the proverbial cucumber. This approach, I thought, would have served Sir Lynden well.

As a leader, Sir Lynden gave the Bahamas at least four great institutions: the College of the Bahamas, now the University of the Bahamas; the National Insurance Board; the Central Bank; and the Defense Force, which remain the cornerstones of his legacy. He also inspired many of our leaders today, one of these being the Rev. Bishop Neil Ellis, who attributes much of his success to the inspiration of Sir Lynden. When reminiscing on the life of Sir Lynden, here is what another religious leader (Lynden's former pastor), Pastor Arthur Roach[4] had to say about the man whom he called "A man of vision and faith." In a reflective mood, Pastor Roach moved into his discussion of Sir Lynden with the following quote from Proverbs 4:3–4:

> 3. For I was a son unto my father, Tender and only beloved in the sight of my mother.

> 4. And he taught me, and said unto me: Let thy heart retain my words; Keep my commandments, and live;[5]

---

4   Information contained in a letter from Pastor Roach to Doctor Rahming.

5   American Standard Version (BibleGateway.com).

According to Pastor Roach, these two passages of scripture, more than any other, sum up the life and legacy of the man who has been dubbed the Father of the Nation.

Pastor Roach goes on to quote Sir Lynden as a university student:

> So with a term of work behind me, I shall now prepare for my first exams in May of next year . . . I hope to complete the whole (by) next year. This will mean a full and rugged schedule, but I'm sure I could do it successfully with God's help. With his help, I shall not fail, and when I return, I'm confident I shall have established a record in more ways than one. My faith is unshaken.

According to Pastor Roach, those words give us insight into Sir Lynden's mind and faith as a young university student. Pastor Roach said, "Indeed, his faith was real and unshaken, and his life was an example of being full of faith and hope."

In the opinion of Pastor Roach, that faith helped the young Lynden to complete his law studies, enter the law profession, and then assured his political career to liberate his Bahamian people and wipe away every tear and make the Bahamas the best little country in this region.

Pastor Roach outlined examples of what this faith brought to the people of the Bahamas: it assisted in ushering in one man, one vote; women's right to vote; and the crowning glory of independence on July 10,1973. It gave us the College of the Bahamas, now the University of the Bahamas, and National Insurance. His faith and faithfulness gave Bahamians the five-day workweek. It allowed Sir Lynden to mix and mingle with all churches and leaders, and finally, it allowed him to renew his own faith and opened the door for his return to the church of his childhood.

Pastor Roach drew on many vignettes to explain his understanding of Sir Lynden. One involved events at the dedication service for the New Macedonia Church building in Kemp's Bay, Johnson's Bay, South Andros, his parliamentary constituency.

According to Pastor Roach, Sir Lynden began his speech with "The first time I heard the word 'Macedonia' was in Sabbath School Class." Pastor Roach went on to say that Sir Lynden was never ashamed of his roots, his spiritual roots in particular. He also mentioned the fact that Sir Lynden's ability to quote the Holy Scripture verses endeared him to many Christian denominations. Hence, he was at home with Baptists, Anglicans, Catholics, Brethren, Church of God, as well as his own Seventh-day Adventists, where, as a preteen, he made an early profession of faith in Christ and was baptized with other church friends.

Pastor Roach shared another interesting fact in the spiritual journey of Sir Lynden. He revealed that with the encouragement of several Adventist Christians, including Ivy Tynes Neblett, who was one of those baptized with him many years before, Sir Lynden experienced a second *Nicodemus baptism* at the Centerville Seventh-day Adventist Church in 1996. There he gave a faithful testimony before many witnesses and ecumenical clergy, parliamentary colleagues, family, friends, and well-wishers. According to Pastor Roach, on his desk in his private law offices, Sir Lynden had a series of tracts entitled "Why I am a Seventh-day Adventist Christian" and "What Is a Seventh-day Adventist?" This was sharing his faith. Not only was this outward display of faith evident, but also his kind and generous heart allowed him to be a regular supporter of humanitarian efforts at in-gatherings as well as tithes and offerings.

As his reflections drew to a close, Pastor Roach, in a somber mood, continued, "When we were told of his illness, a group of pastors and leaders met at his home and had a special prayer and anointing service for the Lord's will to be done. During that prayer and anointing service, there was a loud clap of thunder at the end. Sir Lynden said aloud, 'That's the answer. The Lord has spoken through the voice of thunder.'"

His church community will remember his positive contributions and faithfulness. Unfortunately, in the midst of the positive, there is also some negative. Sir Lynden fed the young in the nest, and his care was such that the young felt as if the nest was the best place to remain. He told them to take flight, but they were content to remain in the nest and be fed. This was a nest that they had already outgrown. In recent times, the majority of the population is now realizing that more persons should have been groomed for leadership positions. Many more should have taken advantage of leadership training.

Not only did we lose the opportunity to capitalize on leadership training, but we also lost out on the proper development of a vital component of our economic sector, the skilled trade profession. When the PLP came to power, many skilled professional workers such as carpenters, masons, and tailors left the workforce to become busboys in the hotels to make a quick dollar.

Early on in his administration, Sir Lynden recognized the destructive path that the youth were traversing and tried to correct this by suggesting the institution of programs such as National Service; but what may have been a worthwhile endeavor never took root, and we may be the worse off for it now. They called it Pindling's Army, and this may have discouraged him from pushing the program forward.

By the mid-1980s, the cry "LO, LO, LO gat to go!" rang out loud and clear. I believe that I was chosen by certain men in the council to aid in the downfall of Sir Lynden. They saw me not only as the president of the council but also as a friend of Sir Lynden, and if the friend could be enlisted to bring about his downfall by delivering the letter, then their task would be complete without a blame or guilt. By not delivering the letter, I believe that I kept a certain degree of needed stability within the country at a time when the world was set to lobby for the freeing of Nelson Mandela, and Sir Lynden played a major part in this process. The letter delivered may have stymied this endeavor.

Sir Lynden was a great leader. He was a man among men. He had an engaging presence, but now we must await the passage of time to vindicate and honor him fully. He was trained in England with men such as Patrice Lumumba, Kwame Nkruma, and Nelson Mandela, men who saw the injustices in their countries and men who wanted to make a difference. Sir Lynden will take his place in history alongside these great leaders. He was a leader chosen for such a time.

The measure of the man can be seen in some of the speeches that he has given over the years. Pay special attention to the speech "I Have Come to Look for America." These are now presented below through the courtesy of the governor-general Lady Marguerite Pindling from a book by Patricia Roker entitled *The Vision of Sir Lynden Pindling: In His Own Words: Letters and Speeches, 1948–1997.*

Small Island States

Mr. President, the peace, stability and security of small island states have been seriously threatened by the drug trafficking barons. The proliferation of drug trafficking continues to represent for much of the world a problem of the most vexing dimensions. The Island States of the Caribbean and the Bahamas straddle the flight paths and sealanes between the narcotics-producing countries of South America and the principal consumer markets on the North American continent and have found themselves, by these geographic circumstances, especially vulnerable to exploitation as transshipment centers for international drug trafficking operations. Archepelagic nations like The Bahamas have been pressed to the outer limits of their financial and security resources in the attempt to sustain effective interdiction and law enforcement measures against this nefarious scourge.

Drug trafficking in the Bahamas became the focus of international attention in the mid 1970's. Two of our major responses to the drug threat were to increase funding to the Police Department and, at the same time, create a coast guard to patrol the seas throughout the Bahamas' archipelago. The budgetary effect of those decisions was to transfer substantial resources from economic and social programmes like education, health and capital infrastructure to combat the escalating drug problem.

In 1975, the total recurrent and capital expenditure on law enforcement was approximately US $9.9 million. Five years later, in 1980, total expenditure rose by over 100% to US$20.2 million. At the end of 1985, total expenditure on law enforcement in the Bahamas is likely to be in the region of US$41.0 million or another 100% increase over the 1980 figure. The numbers speak for themselves. Law enforcement in The Bahamas, as a direct result of drug trafficking, is exacting a tremendous toll on the limited resources of our country.

Mr. President, four weeks ago when the Group of Five met in New York, three weeks ago at the Commonwealth Finance Ministers Meeting in the Republic of Maldives, two weeks ago at the IMF/World Bank Governor's meeting in Seoul, and last week at the Commonwealth Heads of Government Meeting in Nassau, world leaders arrived at the same broad consensus on the current parlous state of global economy: the United States led economic recovery over the past eighteen months produced marginal benefits almost exclusively to the industrialized nations and even in those countries modest economic growth and an abatement in the rate of inflation was achieved in exchange for rising unemployment and/ or increased budget deficits.

The modest improvement in the industrialized countries was also accompanied by an escalation in protectionist sentiments and measures a development which if allowed to proceed unchecked, will certainly impact unfavorable on the terms of trade in developing countries. That would be disastrous, particularly for many of the developing island states in the Caribbean which are still experiencing the adverse effects of the oil shocks of the early 1970's. Moreover, some of these states have not yet recovered from the austerity measures imposed by international institutions as part and parcel of the so-called structural adjustment process.

It would appear therefore, that the currently popular argument that the developed states must first emerge from the recession in order for the developing states to progress is patently false. The reality is that the developing states, particularly small island states, are regressing in the face of advancements by the industrialized nations and, consequently, the economic gap between the two groups is expanding rather than contracting. Indeed, the economic vulnerability of small sates is increasing and precious little is being done by the industrialized counties or the international agencies to reverse this unwelcome trend. (Statement at the Commemoration of the Fortieth Anniversary of the United Nations General Assembly, New York, October 23, 1985)

I Have Come to Look for America

At this momentous time, it is good to be here with you in the heartland of America. It is wondrous to once again walk with the warriors who marched with the Rev. Dr. Martin Luther King Jr., and to see for myself the blossoming reality of his dream. You have built beautiful, caring communities; you have graduated bright, young people into the professions; you have put a Mayor for all into City Hall; and you have had a Presidential candidate that is still standing tall.

I yearn for the day when together we will celebrate the coming of age of real democracy in South Africa. It is for that reason that I have come to look for America. While you in America bask in the sunshine of the summer of your success upside down and halfway round this troubled globe winter has fallen on South Africa.

While the gluttonous tentacles of the money-changer threatens to smother Lady Liberty's Torch of Freedom, South Africa simmers and burns. Today America, land of the free and home of the brave, appears hoodwinked by Boer cunning and blindfolded by Boer censors. As you and I fellowship this morning in the foundry of the Rainbow Coalition, apartheid's gruesome plague festers beneath a pall of blue smoke, suckling at the breast of silence. Oh, say, can't you see the hideous creature of the marriage of riches and racism? It is such an ugly child!

We in the Commonwealth, like you in America, have had ample opportunity to come to terms with the horror which is apartheid. Yet, when our Eminent Persons Group recently finished their mission to South Africa, the first line they wrote was: "None of us was prepared for the full reality of apartheid." The glitter of South African gold and the sparkle of South African diamonds mask the black miner's hair-raising squalor. Iron-fisted repression combined with unconscionable racism, have created surrealistic inequalities. Brothers and sisters, I have come to look for America.

The first goal of Operation Push is a comprehensive economic plan for the development of black and poor people. Your State Department is on record in support of your aims. In its own words, "Economic development is essential, for poverty and social injustice provide Communism the opportunity to provoke violence and subversion." Oh say, can't you see Crossroads? There forty thousand souls sift the winter mud for the remains of their burnt-out lives. There are six times more blacks in South Africa than whites. Yet the system of apartheid, under which blacks are separate and unequal, smashes 25 million suffering souls into less than fifteen percent of the land. This social injustice has guaranteed poverty. Poverty and social injustice have indeed, as your State Department accurately predicted, bred violence. In South Africa there grows an endless litany of the maimed and massacred. Machetes bite flesh, truncheons crush skulls and bullets burst breasts.

Husbands and wives, grandfathers, and grandmothers, children, and infants are beaten, bombed or burned in towns whose names we have had to learn. Names like Sharpeville, Crossroads, Alexandra, Sowetu, Mamelodi and Guguletu, which sound so strange and distant but which, in reality, are no further from Cottage Grove than is Cabrini Green from Cicero. In the dawn's early light, behold the armored personnel carrier bristling with automatic weapons and the ceaseless uncurling of the rubber whip. The armored personnel carrier, which the Afrikaaner calls a casspir, and the hardened rubber whip weighted at the tip ends, which he calls a sjambok, have become the symbols of the determination of the racist minority to confound history.

For hundreds of millions around the world, America still shines as a bright beacon beckoning all who would be free. Yours is a nation forged in revolution, dedicated to freedom and sanctified in battle. Who could count the number for whom the United States Marine has meant deliverance? Who could count the number for whom your Stars and Stripes have meant a new dawn? Who can enumerate those for whom your Lady Liberty has meant sanctuary and your American eagle hope?

So deeply runs the American liberal tradition that you alone among the nations of the world would rather have torn your land apart than see black men in chains. This morning I bring to America's window the manacled black people of South Africa, their bodies bashed and bullet-riddled by their oppressor; their knuckles bloody and raw from knocking on the doors of the world. I have come to look for America; and while here in the land of Lincoln I beg you: Help them please. You can help; I know you can help.

The great liberal tradition of America must now be combined with those similar traditions of the Common-wealth and Western Europe. The countries of the North Atlantic Treaty Organization and the countries of the commonwealth must now collectively raise their arms for freedom to avoid having to later bear arms for justice. Collectively they could bring about freedom and justice in South Africa. "As for you and I, the sons and daughters of the African Diaspora, we must also raise our voices high and tell the Afrikaaner Pharoah: Let our people go! (Address at Operation Push National Convention, Saturday, July 26, 1986)

Apartheid

For years, the Republic of South Africa has been at the centre of international controversy. For years, the international community has been searching for a means by which this racist pariah could be persuaded to embrace democracy. For years, the Government of South Africa has refused. It has ignored entreaty, abused diplomacy and crushed resistance.

Now, in the face of such intransigent brutality, the patience of the international community has all but expired. By the caprice of fate, we here in the Bahamas find ourselves at the centre of an eleventh hour attempt to substitute a day of dialogue for the impending night of blood.

Dialogue is the last hope that now remains for a peaceful solution to the problem in South Africa. The South African Government has made it patently clear that it will not willingly undertake discussions with the legitimate representatives of the black majority in South Africa. It has declared these black leaders to be radicals and communists. It has appealed to the Western community for support in its efforts to dismantle apartheid. But is Nelson Mandela a radical? Is the African National Congress a communist organization? Is the South African Government dismantling apartheid?

Many people know that the most liberal member of the South African Government is more right wing than is Prime Minister Thatcher. Yet, most of us forget to take this into account when we try to understand what State President Botha means when he refers to 'radicals.' The fact is that by the standards of the Afrikaaner Government in Pretoria, Senator Richard Lugar would be a radical and Senator Edward Kennedy a dangerous extremist.

The Suppression of Communism Act, 1950 defines communism as "seeking any form of social, political, economic or industrial change by unlawful acts or omissions, or by means which include the promotion of disturbance or disorder." Whether we believe it or not, it is a "communist act" in South Africa for a black man to marry a white woman. To advocate one man one vote is treasonable and punishable by death. Unfortunately, because many individuals are unaware of the particular meanings these terms bear in South Africa, they have been seriously misled with regard to the motives and actions of black leaders in South Africa.

What then is this thing called apartheid that the whole world now so resolutely condemns? What about this apartheid that has the nations of the world calling for economic sanctions against South Africa? What is the rationale for the sanctions they are imposing? To understand all this it would be necessary to review what apartheid really is and how it really works.

Apartheid is the Africans word for separateness. Most of us have never had to confront its reality accept it as a broad, ill-defined system of racial separation much like segregation in the old American south. It is not! The elements which apartheid shares with segregation are but the tip of the iceberg. Beneath them lies a carefully developed network of hundreds of laws systematically refined to guarantee white supremacy. These laws govern marriage and sexual intercourse, the ownership of land and where to live, freedom of movement and where to work, the right to political expression and the right to vote, the level of education and the right to collective bargaining.

"The Prohibition of Mixed Marriages Act and the Immorality Act outlawed marriage and sexual relations between the races. The Population Registration Act divided the population into racial, ethnic and cultural categories firstly, into "Black," "white," and "coloured" and secondly, the "coloured" were subdivided into "Capecoloured," "Cape Malay," "Indian," "Chinese," "other Asiatic" and "other coloured."

While whites of English, Dutch, Italian, Portuguese and German origin, despite their cultural, linguistic, ethnic and historical differences, were exempted from any sub classification, blacks were not only subclassified but, under Groups Areas Act, were separated into specifically designated areas called "homelands." This Act was the instrument used to give 86.3 per cent of the land to whites and 13.7 per cent of the land to six times as many blacks.

A series of Apartheid Acts of Parliament make it an offense for different races to be educated in the same schools and specify the level of education available to each. A former South African Prime Minister laid down the principle to be applied to educating black South Africans. Speaking at the introduction of his Bantu Education Act he said: "Our school system must not mislead the Bantu by showing him the green pastures of European society in which he is not allowed to graze." Apartheid has meant a systematic denial of educational opportunity for blacks. The top salary for those teaching black students is lower than the lowest salary for those teaching whites. Taxes are imposed on Black Education Authorities with the express intention of making even the limited opportunities too expensive for the masses. Although some companies run remedial courses for their workers, it is an offense to provide night classes for black workers.

The Pass Laws of South Africa are among the most hated elements of apartheid. Although everyone in South Africa must carry an identity card, those of blacks are pasted into a book called a "pass." This pass contains additional information such as tribal group, employer's name and address, length of employment and tax receipts.

Each month the employer of each black South African must sign his or her pass. Whenever employment is terminated the date of the termination must be entered.

The pass of black women also contains the name, address and reference book number of her husband, parent or guardian.

When passes are issued, fingerprints are recorded for a central bureau. All other races must produce a pass within a week of being asked but blacks who cannot produce a pass upon demand may be arrested on the spot. Each year the number of prosecutions for pass law violations average three quarters of a million. Every day about two thousand blacks are picked up for pass law questioning.

The pass laws enable the Government to regulate the movement of black South Africans into so-called white areas and to treat him like an immigrant in his own country.

It is against this background that we must look at the recent "reforms" to determine how far the South African Government has gone to genuinely dismantle apartheid. Far from dismantling apartheid, the much-touted "reforms" are absolutely insignificant as measures to give the vote to black South Africans in the land of their birth. In fact, they constitute, for the most part, refinements to the system of apartheid which strengthens the Government's ability to control the black population and increase the obstacles to a universal franchise. At the same time they have served as most effective sops to international opinion.

Today, the South African propaganda machine once again functions in darkness. Their smear campaigns, paid apologists, and bought newspapers proceed with impunity.

Ladies and gentlemen, time is rapidly running out on apartheid. From Norway to New Zealand the world is gearing up to snuff out the rewards and riches on which it feeds. Up to now South Africa has been perpetrating, with the aid of a sophisticated disinformation campaign, a massive hoax on the Western World. This has been possible because Western participation in the South African economy, together with systematic separation of the two communities in South Africa and relentless manipulation of the domestic media, has shielded the white South African from the consequences of his iniquitous policy.

We in the Commonwealth, having taken the first bold step, have cracked the dam that now protects apartheid. Already, State President

Botha is beginning to feel the cold spray of the dangerous waters. White South Africans are fond of a metaphor that suggests that integrating the society would render the fortunes of the tiny white community awash in a larger black community comparable to the fortunes of a drowning man in 20 or 30 feet of water. Well, today all indications are that the Afrikaner had better learn to swim; and that is the rational for sanctions. (Lecture on the Rationale for Sanctions against South Africa, College of the Bahamas, August 21, 1986)

Sir Lynden died a contented man knowing that he had done all that he could for his country. He had run the course and had finished the race. Some of the last words that he spoke to me were "I shall not die. I shall live. If you die, you cannot help God."

Indeed, I want to believe that Sir Lynden is not dead, for his particular contribution in the defeat of the apartheid system of government will be discussed again and again by generations yet unborn. By extension, in the context of this book, it can be said that if the letter was delivered, Sir Lynden would not have been able to continue to advance the purpose that God had in store for him.

Sir Lynden had a great respect for the Christian Council. He listened to what it said. On many occasions, we would meet on particular concerns such as the D'Arcy Ryan case. Shortly after the meeting, this issue was sorted out. We also met on the introduction of horse and dog racing in the Carmichael area. This idea was abandoned. He called us at times to discuss any number of matters. We now turn to the organization that had the ear and respect of Sir Lynden.

CHAPTER 4

The Bahamas Christian Council

WHAT WE NOW know as the Bahamas Christian Council came into being in the early 1940s and started off as some social gathering for expatriate ministers of religion, in particular. The council was led by a chairman in the person of Rev. William Makepeace of the Methodist Church, and its members included ministers of the Methodist, Presbyterian, Salvation Army, and Anglican denominations. The individual who served as chairman was informally elected and served for a period of one year. The Baptists, even though they formed the largest worship block in the Bahamas at the time, were not participating in this fraternity, which met for discussion and camaraderie. In those war years, the road was not easy for Baptists in the Bahamas, and many times we felt as if we too were on the battlefield. Many times, our efforts as soldiers of the cross were thwarted.

But even with the denominational fractions, the trouble and tragedy of the day served to bring us together as one body. The council began to make its presence felt outside of its functions as a fraternity of ministers, as the effects of the Second World War crept ashore in the Bahamas. By 1942, the Second World War heated up and became more pronounced, making living conditions difficult throughout the world, and the Bahamas was pulled more and more into the fray. It was at this time that the council took on a new role, that of a sentinel, offering ecumenical prayers each day at noon at the Cenotaph downtown.

As the council prayed, the war continued to be waged on many fronts. Citizens and residents of the Bahamas, including myself, were pulled further into the conflict and started contributing to the war effort by collecting scrap iron that was subsequently shipped to England, where it was used in the manufacturing of weaponry.

Around 1943 or 1944, the British Royal Air Force became a fixture within the Bahamas; the winds of war did not pass by the Bahamas. These islands played host to the likes of Heir Wenagren, who was rumored to have had secret ties to Germany as a Nazi sympathizer. It was further rumored that he was actively engaged in the fight against England. Wenagren took up residence at Hog Island, now known as Paradise Island, and befriended the duke of Windsor, who came to the Bahamas in 1942 as governor.

It was said that Wenagren was engaged in a campaign to have the duke reinstated as King of England, even though he had abdicated "for the woman he loved." However, the jury is still out on its determination of whether the Duke of Windsor was exiled from the throne because of his amorous attachment or for his Nazi leanings.

The council continued to hold its daily prayer vigils at the Cenotaph, as aircrafts crash landed in the vicinity of Oakes Field airport on a rather regular basis. There was a wide held local belief that this was the work of sabotage carried out by spies who operated inside the Bahamas. As a young lad, I, among others, benefited from these unfortunate tragedies by collecting the plastic debris from the downed aircrafts, which we later fashioned into finger rings. The council continued to offer prayers as the war years progressed. England and the allied forces were on the losing end.

The most powerful weapon available to the council in those days was prayer, but this weapon was not used to ease the social ills of the community. For example, during the Burma Road riot of 1942, the church and council did not use their voice as a body. For who would speak against the state (government) when the state and church were one and the same. The state held that the workers' pay should not be increased. In any event, only one segment of the community, the black majority, was being affected. Though powerful in number, they were powerless in economic and political clout.

In 1945, we saw the end of war and the prayers at the Cenotaph ceased, but the council remained in existence and still met as a group. In the late 1940s and early 1950s a few Baptist ministers went abroad to further their education with theological training. These men became accepted and well respected within the council and were elected to fill certain executive position. These included men such as R. E. Cooper Sr., A. S. Colebrook, Harcourt W. Brown, and E. C. Grant.

Even though the indigenous Bahamian ministers were becoming bolder in their commentary on social issues, their voices were still not loud enough to make a real difference in times of social unrest, such as Black Tuesday, the day on which Sir Lynden and Sir Milo orchestrated the casting out of the mace and the hourglass from the House of Assembly in protest against the restricted time that was imposed on them to address important issues in parliament. The mace was a symbol of giving the power back to the people, who were left powerless outside its walls. Parliament had no time or concern to address the cries of the majority.

The most we were able to do was offer to the masses spiritual council and lead prayer meetings and vigils that addressed current social issues. At one such meeting, held at Clifford Park, Sir Roland Symonette was in attendance, and he was what we called a good Methodist. For attending this meeting, he was severely reprimanded by fellow colleagues, as he was premier; and the prayer meeting was held by those who were against casino gambling in the Bahamas, which his government supported. By the advent of majority rule in 1967, the Rev. Charles Smith, the then-secretary of the council and pastor of Mount Moriah Baptist Church, left town in 1968 to further his education at Southern Baptist Theological Seminary, as he said that events were getting personally uncomfortable for him as secretary of the council.

Even before he was ordained in 1963, matters were uncomfortable. One such matter was the 1962 general election, which was hotly contested, and it was also the first time that women were able to vote. This election, in my opinion, was lost by the majority because of oversight. The PLP had the popular vote but overlooked the fact that through gerrymandering, popular votes could be conquered by those who captured the majority of seats. The Progressive Liberal Party learned from that mistake, making sure that they won the majority of seats as well as the popular vote during the next general election held in 1967.

Bahamians are world renowned for their zeal in celebrating the Christmas season, but in 1966, there were no Christmas celebrations to speak of. It was the eve of the January 10 elections (1967) that would usher in majority rule. Sir Lynden, thereafter always called elections on months or dates that spoke to the number 10, for example, April 6. Here we have April, which is the fourth month, and the 6 day, 4 + 6 = 10. The date January 19, 1967, was chosen by the leaders of the United Bahamian Party, and its significance did not go unnoticed by a minister from Andros, who, as most in the Bahamas were to learn, contacted the leader of the Progressive Liberal Party telling him to read Exodus 12:1–3:

1.   And Jehovah spake unto Moses and Aaron in the land of Egypt, saying

2.   This month shall be unto you the beginning of months: it shall be the first month of the year to you.

3.   Speak ye unto all the congregation of Israel, saying, In the tenth day of this month they shall take to them every man a lamb[6]

The tenth day of the first month of the year would also mark the freeing of the black majority in the Bahamas from minority rule. The date chosen by the leaders of the United Bahamian Party would be the rallying call for freedom for the Progressive Liberal Party. In 1966, there were no elaborate Christmas celebrations for the members of the PLP, as they were busy on the campaign trail. This paid off with victory at the polls on the tenth day of the first month.

The PLP was ushered in as the government of the Bahamas, as the strains of the song from the movie *Exodus*, "This Land Is Mine," echoed in the hearts, minds, and ears of a jubilant black majority who dubbed Lynden Oscar Pindling "Moses." It should be noted, however, that the PLP did not win the majority through the election. The election was a tie. The two votes that gave the PLP the majority came from two independents: Sir Randol Fawkes, who became the minister of labor; and Sir Alvin Braynen, who became speaker of the honorable House of Assembly. I

---

6   American Standard Version GatewayBible.com.

was privileged to serve as Chaplain to Sir Alvin from 1967 to 1969 before entering Southern Baptist Theological Seminary, Louisville Kentucky.

One year later in 1968, majority rule became more entrenched as another general election was called after the sudden passing of Uriah Mcphee. It has remained a mystery as to the exact day of Mr. McPhee's passing. Did he die on the day that the announcement of his passing was made, or did he die previously, and his passing was kept a secret until the leaders of the PLP were able to formulate an election strategy? This question has never been answered. In 1968, there was a clean sweep, and the PLP emerged as the undisputed ruling party, capturing twenty-eight of the thirty-eight seats in parliament. The black majority was given power and took to flight, literally.

Many traveled to London for the first time for business and pleasure—as if it were as easy as flying to Andros. In my humble opinion, Bahamians came into too much freedom too quickly; we did not make education a priority in guiding people along the lines of what true freedom was. We did not do as good a job as we should have in expanding the base of leadership training to transform more people from followers into leaders. The importance of cultivating proper work ethics was not encouraged. Only a select few who were already prepared were chosen to run and manage the government.

The Baptists were now holding influential positions throughout the council and with Rev. Dr. R. E. Cooper Sr., a top-notch Baptist leader, as president, we were on the move. Rev. Dr. R. E. Cooper Sr. served for two years, and during this time, he became the voice for the moral conscience of the people. Dr. Cooper was an indigenous Christian leader and so was more able to speak and be received by the people with the authority of a son of the soil. Believe it or not, before majority rule, the Baptist church called in foreign ministers to preach at the Baptist Day Annual March. They were hesitant to speak out, lest they offend the powers of the day, namely, the Bay Street Boys, causing their members to be fired from their jobs. Some members were afraid to march for the very same reason.

Dr. R. E. Cooper Sr., who was also the president of the Bahamas National Baptist Missionary and Education Convention, filled the position of chairman of the council. It was during this time that the council drafted its first constitution.

Edwin Taylor, a Methodist minister, led in this endeavor. The aims and objectives of the council as set out in its constitution were as follows:

1. *To promote understanding and trust between the various parts of Christ's Church in the Bahamas at all levels.*

2. *By the joint action of Christians in the Bahamas, further Christ's mission of service.*

3. *To bear witness for the Christian Community in the Bahamas on matters of social or common concern* [7]

Within the constitution, the following Christian denominations could become members of the council:

> Every autonomous body of Christians established in the Bahamas who accept the basis of the Council and all agencies related either to such bodies or whose object is to further Christian work (herein called "member organization") shall be entitled to join the Council, and the heads of such bodies and agencies shall be exofficio member of the Council and shall each be entitled to appoint two ordained persons and two of the laity to represent them on the Council, (all such persons being herein referred to as "members").[8]

Within the constitution of the council is an article that refers to the appointment of commissions:

1. The Council shall appoint such commissions as it shall deem necessary.

2. The purpose of the commissions will be to investigate either such matters as the Council may refer to it or such other matters that fall within its terms of reference and formulate statements thereon for adoption by the Council in general meeting.

3. The Council shall decide whether the statement of any commission shall be adopted or not or the Council may refer such statements to any member body for advice before deciding whether to adopt such decision.

---

7   Printed with permission of Bishop Delton D. Fernander, president Bahamas Christian Council.

8   Ibid.

4. Until the Council decides otherwise the following commissions shall be established: i. Moral and Social Matters ii. Church and State iii. Biblical and Theological Matters iv. Broadcasting (radio and television)

5. The Council shall appoint a chairman for each commission at the Annual General Meeting and the commission chairman shall have the right to select such other members either from the Council or from the public at large to serve on his commission.

6. Any member of any commission shall have the right to refer a question under discussion in a commission to a general meeting of the Council.

7. Each commission shall present to the Annual General Meeting a report of its deliberations during the preceding year.[9]

It was the privilege of the council to plan the independence worship services in conjunction with government officials. We were noticeably included then. We walked on the red carpet at Clifford Park. At the independence worship, the sermon was delivered by the Rev. Dr. R. E. Cooper Sr., president of the Christian Council and president of the Bahamas National Baptist Missionary and Education Convention on Clifford Park.

Reverend Cooper, Baptist, served for one year from 1973 to 1974. Other presidents of the council have been:

1. Rev. Edwin Taylor, Methodist: three years, 1974 to 1977

2. Dr. Philip Rahming, Baptist: three years, 1977 to 1980

3. Bishop W. M. Johnson, Church of God: three years, 1980 to 1983

4. Dr. Philip Rahming, Baptist: three years 1983 to 1986

5. Bishop Albert Hepburn, Pentecostal: three years 1986 to 1989

6. Bishop Ross Davis, Pentecostal: three years 1989 to 1992

7. Rev. Dan Scott, AME Zion: two years 1992 to 1994

8. Bishop Harcourt Pinder, Church of God: one year 1994 to 1995

9. Dr. C. B. Moss, Baptist: one year 1995 to1996

---

9   Ibid.

10. Bishop Harcourt Pinder, Church of God: two years 1996 to1998
11. Dr. Simeon B. Hall, Baptist: three years 1998 to 2001
12. Bishop Sam Green, Baptist: three years 2001 to 2004
13. Dr. William Thompson, Baptist: three years 2004 to 2007
14. Bishop John Humes, Pentecostal: one year 2007 to 2008
15. Dr. Patrick Paul, Assemblies of God: three years 2008 to 2011
16. Dr. Randford Patterson, Cousin McPhee: six years 2011 to 2017
17. Bishop Delton D. Fernander: 2017 -

The responsibility of the presidents was that of making the council the voice for all the Christian bodies in the country.

It was to be the one voice and the channel through which all churches move together, not controlling but informing and inspiring.

I fought to ensure that the focus of the council remained that of Christianity, not to be thought of as the council of churches but as the Bahamas Christian Council. During my presidency, the council continued to make substantive contributions to the spiritual direction of the country, and its presence was sought as a voice at national functions. Some of these included welcoming His Holiness Pope John Paul II of the Roman Catholic church and the archbishop of Canterbury of the Anglican community Robert A. K. Runcie to the Bahamas and the memorial state service for the late Sir Roland T. Symonette, first premier of The Bahamas on March 26, 1980, where I brought condolences. During the state dinner commemorating the tenth anniversary of independence, the president of the Christian Council was given the honor of gracing the meal.

In 1983, at the inauguration ceremonies of the Clifton Pier power station, the president led the opening prayer. In that same year, at the opening ceremony of the new national headquarters of the Bahamas Red Cross, the president also led the prayer of dedication. In 1986, the president was given the opportunity to give the invocation at the eighteenth annual Conference of Caribbean Historians. The president was also invited by private institutions such as Roywest Trust and British American Insurance Company to participate in formal celebrations.

The council also contributed to the resolution of many social issues that arose during this time. One of them was the question of the granting of citizenship to Darcy Ryan. Another issue was the introduction of horse and dog racing in the Carmichael community, which was rejected by the government with the backing of the council. It was felt that this activity would have had a negative influence on the people of this young nation.

One of the greatest roles of the council as the moral conscience of the Bahamas came during the turbulent years of the 1980s that saw the proliferation of the drug trade and the subsequent Royal Commission of Inquiry. When the inquiry came, the honeymoon was over. In my opinion, the true movers and shakers of the Bahamas, those who held the economic strings, were becoming tired of Pindling.

The letter was drafted at this time to weigh him down and unseat him from power. It was meant to put an extra nail into his coffin.

Elections were pending, but they feared it would not be sufficient to put Sir Lynden out of office, thus the letter. The Moses of the masses was being painted as the corrupt pharaoh and puppet of drug lords. At a time, when Pres. Ronald Reagan saw fit to remove Ferdinand Marcos from power in the Philippines, we too were in danger of losing the spirit of our new nation to outside investments and interests.

In the fulfilment of its role as the moral and social conscience of the nation, the Christian council, in my opinion, felt obligated to address negative issues surrounding the leader of the nation, thus the letter. Before more is said about the letter, I deem it necessary to discuss the life and times of a few other young men within the Baptist community who were distinguishing themselves in the Bahamian society.

CHAPTER 5

Baptist Ministers

WE WERE CALLED the three musketeers. The Rev. Charles Smith, Michael Symonette, and I were all contemporaries during the1960s. We were all Baptist ministers serving in different associations and were the best of friends. Charles Smith served in the convention led by the Rev. Talmadge Sands on Shirley and East Streets, Dr. Michael Symonette served under the leadership of Bishop T. E. W. Donaldson, and mine was led by Rev. Enoch Backford Sr. Charles has since deceased. Only Michael and myself are still alive.

In the early years, both Zion and Salem Baptist were pastored by the Rev. Daniel Wilshere, who was later relieved from his pastorate of Zion by the British Missionary Society in England. It was not known for sure why this took place, but it was believed that he refused to join the homeland in its decision to create a theological college in Jamaica. This college, which later became Calabar Theological College, a part of the United Theological College of the West Indies. Charles Smith and I attended in the 1960s. Calabar produced pastors to serve in any area of the Caribbean and the Bahamas, whether they were from that country or not. One branch of the Methodists in the Bahamas follows this practice of placing pastors from other countries within Bahamian congregations.

For example, in the early '70s, Edwin Taylor came from St. Kitts to be chairman of the Methodist church in the Bahamas, where he was welcomed with open arms in churches such as those in Spanish Wells, which were not so accommodating to local black Methodist preachers.

It is interesting to note here that the Rev. Talmadge Sands was a Methodist minister who took over from another Methodist minister, the Reverend Moon. Reverend Moon was serving as interim pastor at Zion in the absence of a British Missionary Society Pastor because there were no white Baptist preachers in the Bahamas. Reverend Sands was trained at the United Theological College in Kingston, Jamaica, which catered to several denominations at various campuses. These included the Baptists, Presbyterians, Methodists, Disciples of Christ, and others. Having completed his training, Reverend Sands returned to Nassau but was refused a pastorship at a Methodist church. At the time, it was being said that he could not receive a pastorship because "he was not white enough."

When Reverend Sands entered the Baptist community as a pastor, he became known as the whitest indigenous Baptist pastor in the country, and this was parlayed into his receiving the opportunity to participate in many of the national religious affairs of the country. For example, he was always present at the annual Remembrance Day Service at the Cenotaph. He had a regular church broadcast on ZNS, was chaplain at the Bahamas General Hospital, and also served on one or two government boards. In the early days, it was advantageous for Reverend Sands not to cling to the over-the-hill Baptists, as he could have lost his sway with the churches recognized by the government.

Meanwhile, Reverend Wilshire, having been dismissed without prejudice from Zion, went to live and worship in Fox Hill, where he was able to regroup and continue his ministry in the Bahamas. His choice of place to worship was Zion Fox Hill, and he took up residence in the home of Deacon John Smith, at the spot on which now stands the police station in Fox Hill. Reverend Wilshire later changed the name Zion Fox Hill to Mount Carey Baptist Church. He named the church after that renowned British Baptist who went on mission to India. It is believed that Reverend Carey is the father of the modern Missionary movement in the world. Reverend Wilshire established a good rapport with the leaders of

Mt. Carey and oversaw the physical extension of the church in a northerly direction. Reverend Wilshire not only found support at Mt. Carey but from a number of churches in Long Island and Exuma as well.

After a successful pastorship at Zion, Rev. Talmadge Sands was succeeded by his protégé, Charles Smith, whom he personally groomed and sent to Calabar College, his alma mater. Approximately two years before Charles Smith went to Calabar, he came to work at the telecommunications department, now called Bahamas Telecommunications Corporation (BTC). At the time, I too was employed there as chief assistant to the accountant, Mr. R. A. C. Roberts, father of Bradley Roberts. We became fast friends, as we were both—one of us at Zion on Shirley Street and the other at Mount Carey in Fox Hill, which was a part of the Bahamas Baptist Union Association of Churches with its headquarters at Salem on Parliament Street, which now serves as the office of an attorney.

When Charles announced that he was on his way to college, I marveled over the fact that he was going to the seminary at such a young age. I said to myself that I would not be able to do likewise, not knowing two years after his leaving for seminary that, I too would be a student at Calabar Theological College. I met Charles at Calabar, where he was now two years my senior at college, even though I was ten years his chronological senior. Rev. Charles Smith graduated in 1963 and began his ministry at Zion two years before my graduation and the start of my own ministry in 1965 at Salem Baptist Mission on Kemp Road.

The third member of the three musketeers was Michael Carrington Symonette, the grandson of A. C. Symonette, the first president of the Bahamas National Baptist Missionary and Education Convention. Reverend Symonette's leader was Bishop Donaldson, who was in charge of the St. John's Particular Native Baptist Society. The word "native" ensured that only sons of the soil could assume the leadership of congregations. We all had different leaders and answered to different conventions, but were the best of friends.

For July 1980, three scholarships were given by the Baptist World Alliance (BWA) for three pastors to attend the annual general meeting in London, Ontario, Canada, and they went to the three musketeers: Michael, Charles, and Philip. This was our first introduction to the Baptist World Alliance, and we were considered the new up-and-coming Baptist pastors at the time. Reverend Smith was able to forge a closer connection with the World Alliance than either Michael or myself by his constant presence at meetings and ended up as one of the vice presidents at large of the BWA. Dr. Symonnette did not continue his association with the BWA, but I have continued to this day to serve on commissions of the alliance such as the Ethics Commission, the Commission for Baptist Outreach, and other denominations worldwide.

It was through this commission that I was privileged to travel to the Vatican, where a seminar on Baptist and Roman Catholic relationships was held in December 2002.

This experience has done much to excite me about faithfulness to God. At the time of the seminar, His Holiness Pope John Paul II was ill, and I was unable to manage an audience with him. During this time, I reflected with pleasure over my having already met him and being given the privilege to welcome him to our shores in the Bahamas on behalf of the Christian Council, where he, like Nicodemus in January 1979, visited us at night. While at the Vatican, our ears were tingling with the rumors of who would succeed His Holiness. Would it be Cardinal Francis Arinze or Joseph Ratzinger?

The Rev. Charles Smith, in his role as pastor of Zion, was accepted as one of the main voices for Baptists in the Bahamas even though the president of the Baptist Convention was the main voice. This was so because Zion was often considered the city church and the church most frequently visited by tourists.

While Reverend Smith made his mark at Zion, I made mine in the broadcasting media. Up until 1967, the religious programs aired over radio Bahamas ZNS were canned programs. This meant that the programs were prepared outside the Bahamas and put on the air with no input by the local churches. For example, the Baptist hour was prepared in Texas. After 1967, a change occurred not only in the governance of the country but also in religious programming on the airways. At this time, I was sent to Jamaica by the Southern Baptist Mission in the Bahamas to study radio and television broadcasting at the Jamaica Broadcasting Company (JBC). While at JBC, I became familiar with the basic rudiments of radio and television broadcasting and in producing and directing television and radio programs.

Following my return, Baptist religious programming on ZNS began to change. The singing and preaching contained in the canned programming remained the same, but the introductions, announcements, and closing were done by me. I was permitted by the Southern Baptist

Mission to do that under the direction and supervision of its representative, the Rev. Ernest Brown, chairman of the local mission in the Bahamas. This opportunity allowed me, by voice, to be known wherever ZNS was heard in the Family Islands as well as in New Providence. When I became president of the council in April 1977, I was already known throughout the Bahamas.

As I reflect on my relationship with Charles Smith and Michael Symonette, I would say that we were good friends. We all helped directly and indirectly in the building up of the nation so that our names and our work and aspirations would always be an inspiration to others. We worked to advance in the ministry and to become what we considered to be the best for the Lord. Charles and I were amazed at how often persons would get the two of us confused, as we were both almost the same in size and stature. Dr. Smith is the father of five sons three are in the ministry. His dear wife Jackie is still with us and very active in ministry. She makes the best cup cakes on this side of Jordan. The Rev'd Dr. Michael Symonette is the father of three sons and two daughters, all of whom are in ministry. He and his dear wife Hilda are still with us and like Jackie, Hilda herself is very active in ministry.

Rev. Charles Smith never declared his political affiliations either to me or to the public. He also did not support any particular political party from the pulpit, as was in keeping with his training. He never openly directed his congregation to vote one way or the other, as it was reported that another one of our senior Baptist ministers was heard saying, "I cannot tell you how to vote but vote right. Now in closing, we will sing number 58, 'All the Way My Savior Leads Me.'"

The slogan of the major political party at that time was "All the Way." As far as I could ascertain, Reverend Smith's relationship with Sir Lynden was cordial and friendly and Zion, being a historic church, was where the government led by Sir Lynden would frequently go for official governmental services. At that time, Reverend Smith never expressed his opinion to me on the findings of the Commission of the Inquiry. We simply never discussed it. He had hinted earlier that a letter was being prepared, which he wanted me to sign. When the letter presented itself, I then knew to what he referred. When the clamor over the letter had died down, he came to me privately this time and said that he was glad that I did not deliver the letter.

Reverend Smith's greatest contribution was the stability and growth that he brought to the congregation at Zion, where young people came in and found encouragement, acceptance, and motivation to strive for and achieve their highest potentials. Many of them are now the professionals and leaders of the day. Reverend Smith also hosted a radio program on ZNS called *Hints for a Happy Home*, where he sought to help maintain and encourage stability and love within the home and in our nation.

He was thought to be an outstanding and energetic religious leader who challenged the status quo. He was a fighter and an overcomer who sought to bring out the best in Bahamians. He and his members sought to do this from his position in the Baptists World Alliance, where he rubbed shoulders with Baptist leaders from around the world.

Dr. Smith represented the Bahamas well. In him, members of the BWA saw youth, promise, courage, and possibility. He was not a visible or active player in the fight for majority rule, but when it came, he was one of the newly trained kids on the religious block along with Michael Symonette and myself.

I will also remember him as one who spoke out against gambling. He was a man of insightful intelligence, once pointing out that there was a difference between politicians and theologians that could be found in our training. He maintained that we were trained in philosophy, and politicians, who were mainly lawyers, were trained in logic. The former were therefore more holistic in their view of the world and human nature and the latter more compartmentalized. That being the case, politicians and men of the cloth attacked problems from different perspectives. Charles challenged that perspective.

When it was all over, the Rev. Dr. Charles Smith came up to me and said, "Phil, I am happy that you did not deliver the letter." I looked at him, and he looked at me. I never asked him why. I felt relieved. To me, it was a welcome statement.

Another player in the saga of the letter was Catholic archbishop Lawrence Burke SJ.

CHAPTER 6

Archbishop Lawrence Burke, SJ

S OME KEY MEMBERS of the Bahamas Christian Council, which included the Rev. Dr. Charles Smith, Fr. Kirkley Sands, and Archbishop Lawrence Burke, who, together, it was alleged by the press as will be outlined in chapter 8, without being authorized by the president, produced the letter intended to reach the prime minister. At this point, I would now like to make reference to some facts about one of the members of the group, as he was singled out to me by a fellow colleague. That member being a Catholic archbishop, the late Lawrence Aloysius Burke, SJ who, in my opinion, was arguably the most prominent among the alleged crafters of the letter.

Larry, as he was affectionately called, was the first person to hold the title of archbishop of the Roman Catholic Church in the Bahamas, which was elevated to an archdiocese by Pope John Paul II in 1999. From the time of his ordination as bishop in the Bahamas in 1981 up until his return to his native Jamaica in 2004, I considered Archbishop Burke to be one of the most informed and influential members of the clergy in our nation.

During the time of the Commission of Inquiry, there seemed to have been in my estimation a noticeable camaraderie between Archbishop

Burke and the pastor of Zion Baptist Church, the Rev. Dr. Charles Smith. It blossomed to the point where Archbishop Burke preached in Zion's pulpit. Archbishop Burke was a Jesuit, and it was his membership in that fraternity that made his presence within the group drafting the letter standout. I was cautiously, wisely, and privately informed by a colleague about the historical influence of the Jesuits in overturning governments. Later, my research into this claim led to the following revelations:

> In a book entitled *Daniel: Understanding the Dreams and Vision* by Charlene R. Fortsch,[10] the author places at the feet of the Society of Jesus, the Jesuits, acts of insurrection against religious movements and world governments. Fortsch identifies the genesis of the Jesuits as the early 1550s, when it was formed in response to the Reformation movement. She claims that its main function was to see the demise of the Reformation movement (p. 211).[11]

As the centuries progressed, the power of the Jesuits increased. Fortsch quotes Boyd Barrett in the *Jesuit Enigma* (p. 209) as saying: "The Jesuit order at last reached the pinnacle of its power and prestige in the early eighteenth century. It had become more influential and wealthier than any other organization in the world. It held a position in world affairs that no oath- bound group of men has ever held before or since . . . nearly all the Kings and Sovereigns of Europe had only Jesuits as directors of their consciences so that the world of Europe appeared to be governed by Jesuits only" (p. 212).[12]

In the opinion of Fortsch, the world at that time was ruled by the Society of Jesus, SJ. She goes on to say that at this juncture, the sovereigns of the world became weary of the power that the Jesuits were wielding,

---

10   https://books.google.bs/books?id=UYGDFHov1b8C&pg=PA212&lpg=PA212&dq=the+jesuit+order+r eached+the+pinnacle+of+its+power&source=bl&ots=i1ACBLGX3e&sig=b WQ0JcjKk4IUDGrgYawuSp1oJc&hl=en&sa=X&ved = 0ahUKEwiCy4KPnf LVAhVBQiYKHYj CVIQ6AEIJjAA#v=onepage&q=the%20jesuit%20order%20reached%20the%20pinnacle%20of%20its%20power&f=false

11   Ibid.

12   Ibid.

and some went so far as to ban the order. This occurred in nations such as Portugal, France, and Spain (p. 212).[13]

Here is what has been said throughout the centuries in reference to the Jesuits and their quest for power and control.[14]

John Adams, the second president of the United States, expressed a very strong negative opinion of the Jesuits, which he claimed was backed up by irrefutable evidence.

Napoleon Bonaparte expressed doubts as to whether the order was a religious fraternity. He rather referred to them as a military organization whose aim was world domination.

An English priest by the name of Henry Garnet of the Jesuit order was believed by authorities to be involved in the infamous Guy Fawkes Gunpowder Plot.[15]

In my research, I discovered that the Jesuits is the only religious order in the Catholic church that has been expelled from any country because of its interference in politics. In my opinion, historically, political power and influence formed one of the main features in the plans of the Jesuits, so you may imagine why I hesitated to give the letter any support suspecting the possible influence of its authorship, which included Archbishop Burke SJ.

At the time the events surrounding the letter unraveled, the Bahamas had been independent for only a decade, and Archbishop Burke had been in the country for only three years. I could not shake the feeling that something was amiss. Here was a man who, in my opinion, knew very little of our country's struggles, and of the man who was Sir Lynden but felt he knew enough to get himself on a team destined to question the commitment, direction, and hope for the future success of the nation that Prime Minster Pindling led. My observations concerned me deeply.

Archbishop Burke came to this country at a time when persons thought that Sir Lynden's leadership and character were at their most assailable. In fact, many thought he would not win the election in 1987, but he did.

---

13   Ibid.

14   https://www.scribd.com/doc/30408550/Quotes-About-the-JesuitOrder-From-Famous-People.

15   https://www.bl.uk/collection-items/the-trial-of-henry-garnet-1606.

We were only a decade into independence. We were a young, hopeful, and maturing country, and I could not justify allowing the archbishop, along with the others, to interfere with the political process of our young, vibrant nation.

CHAPTER 7

The Gatekeeper

THE REV. DR. Martin Luther King Jr., in a speech he delivered in Detroit, 1963, said that if a man hasn't discovered something he will die for, he is not fit to live. Throughout the years, I have been blessed to have discovered that thing for which I would be willing to die, and it is that which has become my life's work: I have dedicated my life in the service of Christianity, education, and country.

In defiance of the popular belief that "nothing good can come out of Fox Hill," I was blessed to have penned not only the Pledge of the Commonwealth of the Bahamas but also its national song, "God Bless Our Sunny Clime," in my quest to serve my country. These two contributions are listed among the ten national symbols of the Bahamas. "God Bless Our Sunny Clime" was written and submitted to be the national anthem for the Bahamas and was judged first runner-up. It was subsequently chosen to become the national song.

The Pledge of the Commonwealth of the Bahamas

I pledge my allegiance to the flag and to the Commonwealth of the Bahamas for which it stands. One people united in love and service.

I am a Bahamian nationalist to the core. Not many persons can claim to have been so deeply inspired by love of country to have penned not one but two works of national importance. At the time when I wrote both the pledge and national song, I was a student at the Southern Baptist Theological Seminary in Louisville, Kentucky.

The National Song: "God Bless Our Sunny Clime"

God bless our sunny clime spur us to heights sublime To keep men free. Let brothers, sister stand Firm, trusting, hand in hand thro' out Bahamaland One brotherhood, one brotherhood.

Let gratefulness ascend, courageous deeds extend

From isle to isle. Long let us treasure peace

So may our lives increase, our prayers never cease.

Let Freedom Ring! Let Freedom Ring!

The long, long night has passed, the morning breaks at last

From shore to shore. Sunrise with golden gleam,
Sons, daughters, share a dream, for one working team
One brotherhood, One brotherhood.
Not for this time nor for this chosen few alone
We pledge ourselves. Live loyal to our God, Love country,
friend and foe, oh help us by thy might, Great God our King!
Great God our King!

I entered this "sunny clime" in the quaint village of Fox Hill on January 28, 1933. I was born to Arthur Horatius (Lennie) Rahming and Rebecca Ferguson Rahming and was given the name Philip, the name of my paternal great-grandfather. This, however, is up for debate as those on my maternal side of the family maintain that an old female evangelist looked upon me not long after my birth and called me, "Philip the Deacon," being one of the seven deacons, for those who don't know.

As a Youth in Fox Hill

My exact place of birth was Rose Street off the Fox Hill main road, opposite Romer Street. Coincidentally, the company that came to be my first place of employment, Batelco (BTC), erected an office on the land immediately east of the property formally owned by my maternal grandmother, Jane Sears Ferguson, where I was born. The four-room stone-wall house is no longer there.

Though born at this location, I grew up on the main Bernard Road, in a house that was set back from the road between two large silk cotton trees. This property is about two hundred feet east of Macedonia Baptist Church.

When I was born, my mother feared that I was too tiny to live, but here I am at eighty-four years of age and going strong. Lives and destinies are in the hands of God.

My parents lived to see me become the president of the Bahamas Christian Council, which allowed me to be the chief spokesman for the Christian church in the Bahamas. As president, one of my greatest privileges was to welcome Pope John Paul II to the Bahamas on behalf of the Christian church in January 1979. My parents also lived to see me acknowledged as the author of the national pledge and the first runner-up in the national anthem competition with the song "God Bless Our Sunny Clime."

The name Rahming, which I am privileged to carry, is one of the well- known names in Fox Hill. My great-great-grandfather Guilliam Rahming came from Nigeria via Guyana, South America. He came and lived in the settlement of Fox Hill and was an outstanding man in the community as witnessed by the fact that his obituary was published in the

August 27, 1898, issue of the *Nassau Guardian*. This article stated that he had lived in the area since 1837, three years after Emancipation.

One of Guilliam Rahming's sons, Moses Rahming, was the fifth pastor of Mount Carey Baptist Church, which was built in 1843. He pastored from 1877 to 1900. I became the twelfth pastor serving from 1990 to 2000.

My first alma mater was the Sandilands All Age School, now called Sandilands Primary School. My early teachers included Miriam E. Roker, JP, and the late Ena Bailey and Millicent Ferguson.

Before leaving Sandilands All Age School at the age of fourteen, the mandatory leaving age, I was stricken with typhoid fever. At the time of my illness, I had become the head boy of the school and was unable to deliver my speech at graduation due to the illness, which, in those days, either crippled or killed. The doctor informed my parents that I would not survive, but if I did, I would be of no use to myself. He told them to take their minds off me. Miraculously, however, I recovered and led the life of a normal child. A nurse told me that as I was emerging from a long state of unconsciousness during my hospitalization, I was repeating the twenty-third Psalm.

I must pay my respect at this point to one of my mentors during my closing years at Sandilands All Age School—Carlton E. Francis BA, MA, B.Ed., former honorable minister of finance in the Progressive Liberal Party Government and later pastor of Kemp Road Union Baptist Church. He introduced me to the world of academics and enabled me to begin to walk in that world.

Upon recovery from my illness, I continued my schooling by attending evening classes in the Oakes Field area in the location of the present C. C. Sweeting High School. There, I studied the Junior Cambridge and O levels while working at the Telecommunications Government Department (now BTC). I worked there for thirteen years, first as a wireless telegraphist for five years and then, in the remaining eight years, as an accounts clerk. My success at further studies came through evening classes in mathematics, and this made possible my transfer from telegraphy into accounts. At this time, Mr. Cyril Bowen was the chief accountant at the Telecommunications Department located at the time on East Street North. The results of our studies in terms of our grades were sent to him, and if we did, well, we would receive a scholarship. He noticed that a Rahming from Fox Hill was getting good grades in math, and he remembered another Rahming who had helped him when he was a youngster. He told me that his heart was touched when he saw this Rahming doing so well, and he wanted to return the kindness that he got from one Rahming to another Rahming. He finally called me, and we spoke, and I found out that it was my grand uncle who was the Rahming who had helped him. So he thought to help me in return and thus my transfer from telegraphy into accounts.

After working for eight years in this section, I resigned as chief assistant to the accountant, Mr. R. A. C. Roberts, at a time when I was up for promotion. The director of the telecommunications department, Mr. Kenneth R. Ingraham, an influential person in my life who challenged me to do the best I could and assured me that I could achieve greatness, and other senior heads of departments encouraged me to stay on. I thanked them, but I still had to leave. My resignation was based on a call from God to enter the Christian ministry as a Baptist minister, preacher, and pastor.

To achieve this goal, I entered Calabar Theological College, Kingston, Jamaica, in September 1961. At Calabar, I received my diploma in theology in 1965. On the twenty-second of August 1965, I was ordained as a Baptist clergyman; and in October of the same year, I was installed as pastor of Salem Union Baptist Mission Church, Kemp Road, where I served until the spring of 1969. It was never my intent to end my educational pursuits with a diploma in theology, and I yearned to pursue further studies, but financial constraints prevented the fulfilment of this dream. It was at this point that God once again performed a miracle, and I was given an opportunity to study at Southern Baptist Theological Seminary in Louisville, Kentucky.

One morning, while I was at home in Fox Hill, the phone rang, and the person at the other end said, "Is that you, Brother Rahming? This is Dr. William Graves, the vice president of Southern Baptist Theological Seminary, Kentucky. Would you like to attend our institution?"

I replied, "Yes, sir, but I have no money."

His answer was "I did not ask you that. Do you want to come?"

I again replied, "I have no money."

He again asked, "Do you want to come?"

More than elated, I shouted, "Yes, sir! What do I need?"

The seminary supplied all that I needed. They provided all the college-required forms that I needed to travel with and all the finances for tuition. The officials at the embassy were shocked as I had been trying without success previously to enter the United States to further my studies. I was on my way. I never fully understood how Dr. Graves found out about my interest in furthering my studies, but all I can say is that my acceptance had the hand of God written all over it. At Southern Baptist, I received a masters of divinity degree and a postgraduate masters in theology degree.

Looking back, I believe that it was Rev. Ernest Brown, the Southern Baptist Missionary here at the time, who knew of my desire and dilemma and made a call for me but never told me.

Upon completion of my studies, I returned to the Bahamas in May of 1971 and was employed at the Bahamas Teacher's College, which became the College of the Bahamas in 1974 and later the University of the Bahamas in 2016, until 1993, when I resigned. That same year, I entered the United Theological Seminary in Dayton, Ohio, where I studied and received a doctor of ministry degree in 1996. My thesis was "Transferring the Wisdom, Mores and Culture of one Generation to the Next." My mentors were Rev. Dr. Jeremiah Wright, Dr. Molefi Kete Asante, and Dr. Cornel West.

In April 1977, I was elected and served as the third president of the Bahamas Christian Council, Dr. R. E. Cooper Sr., MBE being the first and the reverend Edwin Taylor, a Methodist, being the second. It was during my tenure as the third president of the council in 1979 that I welcomed His Holiness Pope John Paul II to the Bahamas, at the Queen Elizabeth Sports Centre, now named the Thomas A. Robinson Sports Centre, on behalf of the Christian church. After my one-minute welcome to His Holiness, he stood and beckoned me to him. He embraced me and said some brief words of thanks.

In 1983, I met with the archbishop of Canterbury, the Rt. Hon. Robert A. K. Runcie, during his visit to Nassau.

To date, I, along with the Rev. Dr. Randford Patterson have been the longest serving presidents of the council. I served from 1977 to 1980 and from 1983 to 1986. In addition, I have served as vice president from 1982 to 1983 and from 1992 to 1994.

Presently, I serve as pastor of Rehoboth Ministries and host of the Outreach Radio Program *Light in the Night* aired on Love 97 FM weekly. I also write a weekly column in the *Bahama Journal* entitled "Light in the Night." My other duties include being vice president at large of the Bahamas National Baptist Missionary and Education Convention and member of the Baptist Doctrine and Interchurch Cooperation Commission of the Baptist World Alliance. I am a former member of the Ethics Commission of the Baptist World Alliance (BWA). In January 2016 I was placed on the Queen's honor list with the designation, Officer of the British Empire (OBE).

The BWA is a gathering of Baptist churches, represented by their leaders from around the world. We attend annual gatherings and seminars of rejuvenation and reflection. Attending these annual gatherings has taken me over the years to all the continents and, in some cases, more than once.

This included a visit to South Africa during the last year of Mandela's presidency. We went there to pay him a courtesy call, but unfortunately, he had to leave the country, and he left Bishop Desmond Tutu to meet with us.

I regret not meeting Mandela in his homeland as president. That was during the time when the country was in the midst of the Truth and Reconciliation exercise. However, I did get to meet him when he came to thank Sir Lynden for his help. Pindling was not prime minister then, and the visit, to my way of thinking, was low-key.

Over the years, I have had the honor and privilege to attend the National Prayer Breakfasts in Washington DC. My attendance began during the presidency of Ronald Reagan. I have attended these breakfasts under the presidencies of George W. Bush Sr., Bill Clinton, G. W. Bush Jr., and Barack Obama in 2013.

In 1968, I was appointed justice of the peace and, in May of 2001, received the Humane Letters Degree from Sojourner Douglas College Nassau, Bahamas. I am also the recipient of an honorary doctor of divinity degree from Simmons University Louisville, Kentucky. In 1974, this citation was prepared and delivered by Dr. Duke K. McCall, former president of Southern Baptist Theological Seminary, who has also served as president of the Baptist World Alliance.

My portfolio includes a position as chaplain to the speaker of the honorable house of assembly, at the beginning of majority rule in January of 1967 and a former member of the advisory panel for the Templeton Foundation Prize for Progress in Religion. I was also the second chairman of the National Tourism Achievement Award (NTAA), which is now the Cacique Award in the Ministry of Tourism.

As a Baptist at large, part of my responsibility to the Bahamian religious community was in ecumenical work. Working with the churches and being on ZNS regularly gave me a good opportunity to be in touch with and to make contributions to as many of our churches as possible. I was better known by my voice than by my physical form by persons on our Family Islands.

My active participation in seminary life began in September 1961, during my studies in Jamaica at Calabar. On weekends, I served as president of the Gordon Somers Society, which consisted of a group of students from many different colleges such as nursing, business, education, and theology.

I served as the secretary to the Student Christian Movement (SCM) at Calabar. In 1962, I represented the SCM of Calabar at a conference held in Mexico City. There were at least forty-two denominations represented, and these were vibrant students. The aim of SCM is to work toward people becoming believers or Christians across the board. When we left college, our mandate was to take the message to all and to keep our relationships going. The SCM is a member of the World Federation of Christian Fellowship.

We as members of the SCM left our respective institutions filled with enthusiasm to lead our brothers and sisters to Christ and to maintain a relationship for peace and progress wherever we would go. We were determined to network to keep the fellowship and ideals alive. So when I became employed at the Teacher's College in the Bahamas, I was properly placed to continue the work of SCM among budding teachers who would go out into our schools and carry the message.

Some of these students of the SCM have gone on today to become principals, and they have kept the SCM alive in the high schools and even in some junior schools of the Bahamas. SCM is also in some of the primary schools. SCM is quite alive today in the Bahamas. The current and outstanding national president is Minister Dianna Francis of First Baptist Church, Market Street. I am humbled to know they gave me the credit for the establishment of SCM in the Bahamas.

As far as Christian organizations go, I am also proud of the fact that I was president of the Gordan Somers Society (GSS) in Kingston, Jamaica. The GSS was a fellowship of students studying in Jamaica. Caribbean students came from Barbados, Panama, Nevis, and St. Kitts, Grenada, the Turks and Caicos Islands, the Bahamas, and many other countries in the Caribbean.

Not only have I been spreading the Word of God orally, but I have also been doing it in print. I have written four books as well as many articles for publication. My books include *A New Beginning*, written in 1973 as a tribute to the Bahamas's independence. At the time of independence, I was an executive member of the Bahamas Christian Council and participated in the Independence Ecumenical Service held at Clifford Park.

The president of the council was the Rev. Dr. R. E. Cooper, Sr., a Baptist minister who preached the sermon. Cooper was the last chairman of the Bahamas Christian Council and was named the first president at the stroke of midnight on July 10, 1973. He was no longer chairman, but now president. The council felt that since it was to assume the role formally executed by the Anglican church in a Colonial Bahamas, the leader in an Independent Bahamas should be called president. Reverend Cooper became the chief religious spokesman for the church in an independent nation.

I remember that historic occasion as if it were yesterday. President Cooper's text was taken from 1 Peter 2:9: "But ye are a chosen generation, a royal priesthood, a holy nation, a peculiar people; that ye should shew forth the praises of him who has called you out of darkness into his marvelous light." Oh, if only we had kept that message to heart all these years since it was first delivered! His Royal Highness Prince Charles was present among so many others. He made favorable private comments to Dr. Cooper about his sermon.

My second book, *Martin Luther King Jr., His religion, His Philosophy*, was published in 1986. In 2002, the book *A Guide to Church Membership*, a handbook for new converts in a Baptist church, was published. My most recent work was published in 2005, *The Pledge of The Bahamas: Its History*.

The Pledge of The Bahamas: Its History was written as a special contribution to the Bahamian community on the history of the national pledge and national song. I also wrote this particular book to add my voice to the many voices who have contributed to the national development of the Bahamas. Many of these voices have been silenced by death without the upcoming generations being made aware of our contributions.

I am grateful to God who has enabled me to pen the national pledge, which the people of the Bahamas will use when saluting the flag of the Bahamas.

Looking back, I thank God for the snow that fell on that cold day in Louisville, Kentucky, when the pledge was penned. I was to attend a two-hour-long Hebrew class but skipped it because of the snow. Because of the snow and the dull grayness of that day, I had no wish to tackle Hebrew. I stayed at home and thought of the "sunshine and the beautiful climate" of the Bahamas.

I thought of home, Fox Hill, New Providence, Bahamas. I thought of the sunshine and the fine weather. It was February 1970, and out of the blue, independence for my wonderful nation came into my mind.

When I left home in August 1969, it was two years after majority rule in the Bahamas. The majority rule being that the 85 percent black population voted in a black majority government for the first time in its political history. This brought an end to the 15 percent white population capturing the majority of seats in parliament. The slogan of the government of the day was "All the Way." The idea of independence was being seriously tossed about and around in the Bahamas at that time. As a matter of fact, a green paper on independence was crafted and being discussed. This green paper was the preliminary outline of a proposed constitution for an independent Bahamas.

In addition, during my years at Calabar, Baptists studied with students from the Presbyterians, Moravians, Methodists, and Disciples of Christ denominations and others. All students at Calabar knew who the outstanding clergymen in the various denominations were at the time. One such star, was the Rev. Hugh Sherlock. He was a Jamaican and past chairman of the Methodist Church in Jamaica and had moved on to become the first president of the conference of the Methodist church in the Caribbean and the Americas. Reverend Sherlock wrote the words for the national anthem of his country. Jamaica became independent in 1962. I felt spellbound at the thought that I, a Bahamian Baptist minister, could find myself following this Methodist minister in crafting the national anthem of my country.

Furthermore, I was mindful of what Dr. Martin Luther King Jr. said in the 1960s during the Civil Rights Movement in America; the Church should be the headlight and not the taillight in the community. I felt that the Bahamas could benefit from the theological and spiritual grounding inherent in such a song composed by a Christian minister.

There and then, I became a captive to some compelling and creative thoughts. I soon began to receive from above the words for the song "God

Bless Our Sunny Clime," and from that song, a pledge which eventually became the Pledge of Allegiance to the Flag of the Bahamas was born. In about twenty minutes, the song was written, and I felt a definite sense of fulfilment.

The next thing was to have the words set to music. In my mind and even out loud, I was singing the song to the tune of "God Save Our Gracious Queen"—not original, but familiar. Even though I had a certain level of expertise in music having begun to play the organ at the age of fifteen and at one time studying with the famous Meta Davis, I felt that I needed to enlist the talent of others. I contacted Professor Dr. John Philip Landgrave, and he put music to the words.

This was then mailed to the Bahamas Cabinet even before the competition for a national anthem was announced. In 1971, when I returned home, the competition was on for a Bahamian National Anthem. I then learned that the competition called for the words as well as the music to be written by a Bahamian. Because Dr. Landgrave was not a Bahamian, I had to seek out a Bahamian composer for the song.

I readily sought Mr. Timothy Gibson who, in a day or so, wrote the music for "God Bless Our Sunny Clime." Gibson suggested that E. Clement Bethel should also have a look at it to make any necessary changes. Bethel did, and his contribution is the musical chord at the end of the second line of each verse.

I am eternally grateful to the generosity of Mr. Timothy Gibson, who himself had entered the song "March on Bahamaland" in the competition. That song became the national anthem of the Bahamas with "God Bless Our Sunny Clime" coming in as the first runner-up in the competition.

In time, I have become to Mr. Gibson, OBE, what Samuel F. Smith is to Francis Scott. You see, Francis Scott wrote the American national anthem "The Star-Spangled Banner" and Samuel F. Smith wrote the National Song, "My Country, 'Tis of Thee." Mr. Gibson wrote "March on Bahama Land," and I wrote "God Bless Our Sunny Clime."

As mentioned before, the pledge came naturally out of the song. My aim in the composition of the song was to reach up to the top, but in composing the pledge, I took pains in reaching down, shaping, and cutting the total number of words. I knew that there were only fifteen words in the British pledge and felt that I should keep the number of words in this pledge to as few as possible.

The pledge recognizes the fact that we are an archipelagic nation but one people, one country, one Bahamas. Then emphasis is placed upon service. In the Bahamas, we have a service industry, and we must serve well. Being united in love, we serve to the honor and glory of God and for the benefit of the people of our Bahamas.

We are one people united in love, and we pledge to serve one another whenever and wherever for the continuing growth, development, and well- being of the people of the Bahamas. We risk failing and possible disintegration if we would accept the convenience and practice of division among ourselves, but a holistic view and adherence to the path will lead us from level to level of understanding, peace, and progress.

Although written without any reference to the preamble to the constitution of the Bahamas, the pledge reflects the high ideals contained therein. For through love and service, the pledge advocates "national commitment to Self-discipline, Industry, Loyalty, Unity and respect for Christian values and the Rule of Law" (preamble to the constitution of the Bahamas, https://www. bahamas.gov.bs). In serving, we will enable and empower our brothers and sisters.

In the 1980s, the Teacher's Association requested that the words "under God" be included in the pledge. They claimed that God was left out, but when the pledge refers to "One people united in Love and Service," I acknowledged God. The "being united in love" is the Agapeic (Agape) love. It is the disinterested love or the love of God who loves not because of but in spite of. Being driven by this love, service will be the product, and it will unite us. Love is the instrumental power to serve, and it will make us our brother's brother.

The pledge was officially selected and approved by the government of the Bahamas on March 21, 1978. On May 6, 1978, the *Nassau Guardian* printed the following under the caption, "Pledge of Allegiance when saluting The Flag":

> I pledge my allegiance to the Flag, And to the Commonwealth for which it stands. One people united in love and service.

"Of the Bahamas" was added later to make the pledge read "To the Commonwealth of the Bahamas."

The pledge, being officially selected and approved five years after independence, led me to conduct some research. I researched the pledge of the United States of America and was fascinated by what I found. The American pledge was written in August 1892. That was a total of 116 years after the independence of the United States of America in 1776. A Baptist minister who was pressured to leave his church, Francis Bellamy (1855–1931) wrote the American pledge. The Bahamian pledge was written by Philip Rahming, who was also a Baptist minister pressured to leave his church. Like me Francis Bellamy was also active in education.

I thank God for the snow and for the fear of Hebrew class, which kept me at home, unplanned, to come up with a contribution that eventually placed me into the history books of my country. It is true that I was inspired by the example of the Reve. Hugh Sherlock, a Jamaican Methodist minister, and equally inspired by the Rev. Dr. Martin Luther King Jr.; but truly, there was a deeper and more special motivation that was placed on me as a child. Folks would always say of Fox Hill, "Can any good thing come out of Fox Hill?" I felt that even as a child, one day, Fox Hill people would rise and change that. I longed to be among that group of persons who would bring about that change. To God must be given all the glory for this great contribution through one of his servants, a son of Fox Hill.

When I look back on my life and the many paths that I could have taken, I am forced to reflect upon certain highlights in world history. I reflect upon the fact that if Rosa Parks had capitulated and given up her seat on that Montgomery bus, the Civil Rights Movement, as we know it, may never have been born; or if Dr. Martin Luther King Jr. had accepted the offer to pastor that congregation in Massachusetts, he may not have been available to lead the Civil Rights Movement in the South.

Had I accepted the call to pastor the church in Missouri in 1971, with the usual care that accompanied the call, then many of the later contributions that I made to my beloved Bahamaland may not have come to pass. This was the thought that sustained me as the media had its say.

CHAPTER 8

The Media Has Its Say

O N MAY 24, 1985, one of the daily newspapers, the Tribune, had as a headline, "Why BCC Chief Didn't Sign, Give Letter to PM." In this article, Athena Damianos attempted to walk the corridors of my mind in an effort to ascertain why the letter was not delivered. She reported that I told a council meeting that my conscience would not allow me to sign a letter addressed to the prime minister. She went on to give her synopsis of the letter saying that it was drafted by a committee on behalf of the council in February and that it expressed concerns over political tension that arose as a result of the Commission of Inquiry report, which found widespread corruption reaching cabinet level.

She went on to say that I was given a mandate to sign the letter and that a meeting was to be arranged between church leaders and Prime Minister Lynden Pindling, but the letter was never signed, and there was no meeting.

The reporter further concludes that at a meeting called to deal with the matter, I said that I had great reservations about the letter because I felt that it did not show proper respect to the prime minister, not to mention the inquiry was over, and he was not judged guilty.

In providing a context for the drafting of the letter, Ms. Damianos, in her article, comments on the findings of the Commission of Inquiry, which included the fact that the findings resulted in noisy street demonstrations at the beginning of the year (1985). She also reports on the fact that at the meeting called to discuss the letter, I was asked why I had allowed three months to go by after the findings of the commission were made public without stating my position.

As stated by the reporter, a committee comprised of Catholic Bishop Lawrence Burke, Rev. Dr. Charles Smith (Baptist), and Rev. Kirkley Sands (Anglican) drafted the original letter that I never brought to the floor of the council for approval.

CHAPTER 9

The Commonwealth Heads of Government Meeting

IN HER REPORT, Ms. Damianos mentions other members of the council whom she endeavored to interview to find out information about the letter.

Among those interviewed was Rev. Albert Hepburn, the then-vice president who, according to Damianos, maintained that he had no knowledge of the letter. Being pressed by the reporter Reverend Hepburn, as reported in the article, stated, "I definitely have no information to give on any letter."

Ms. Damianos also contacted Rev. Ruth Bastian, the newly elected secretary, concerning the letter. Reverend Bastian as well disavowed any knowledge of the letter. The reporter goes on to say that various members of the council were enquiring as to whether or not various churches had met to discuss the letter. She quotes one such member as saying, "The members they have delegated as their representatives on the Council have not dealt with this so the leaders of the Church should step in."

A few days later, on May 29, 1985, the following headline appeared in the press under the byline of Anthony Forbes: "Baptist leader urges govt. to call elections." I, along with high-ranking government officials, including the then-leader of the official opposition, the late Sir Kendal Isaacs, were in the congregation on that day when the Rev. Charles Saunders, pastor of Salem Baptist Church and president of the Bahamas Missionary and Education Convention, made the call for the government to take the issue of the findings of the Commission of Inquiry to the people in the form of a general election.

Rev. Dr. Saunders called on the Bahamas Christian Council to mirror the actions of its counterpart, the Jamaica Council of Churches that called on prime minister Edward Seaga and call for our prime minister Sir Lynden to hold a general election.

While the media storm was brewing, I remained focused that the letter was questionable as to the real purpose and intent of such. I was only driven by the thought of the well-being of everyone rather than the fire of persons whose desire might have been contrary to mine. I wanted peace and calm, and I believed it was possible, so I waited in silence, not so far as inaction but action in silence.

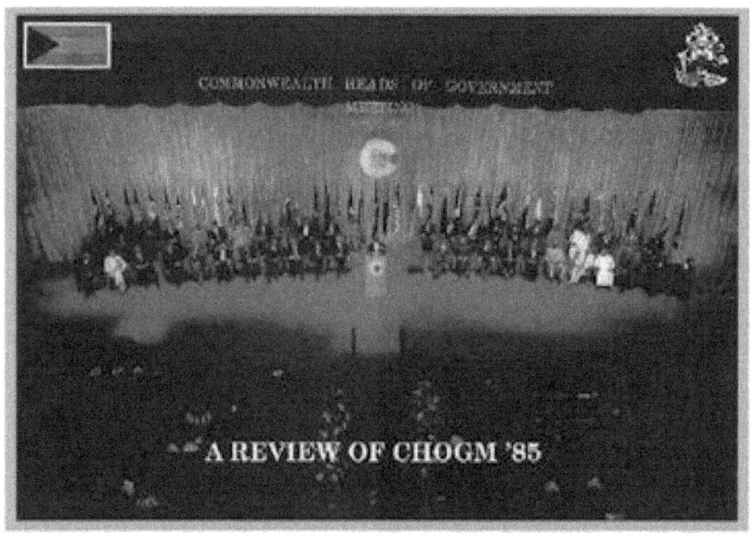

(With the compliments of the director of the
Department of Archives, Bahamas)

Between October 16 and 22, 1985, the Bahamas was host to one of the most historically significant Commonwealth Heads of Government Meetings (CHOGM). This was to be its eighth meeting, and it was hosted by Sir Lynden. It was at this meeting that the fate of the South African government and its stance on apartheid was determined. Sir Lynden played a major role in this process.

In retrospect, I believe that my delivery of the letter would have derailed this divine process that was destined to unfold. I was not to be the only one to hold that opinion. Sir Lynden Pindling provided mentorship to persons who are considered to be the present-day economic "movers and shakers" of Bahamian society.

One such person whom Sir Lynden helped shape and form is Sir Franklin Wilson, chairman of Arawak Homes, and F. R. Wilson & Co. Ltd. Sir Franklin weighs in on the significance of the 1985 session of the Commonwealth Heads of Government Meeting (CHOGM), adding credence and support to my gut feeling years ago that to deliver the infamous letter may have served to rock the boat as it sailed over the waters of freedom for Nelson Mandela and the disenfranchised blacks of South Africa.

Here is what Sir Franklin Wilson had to say in the movie *On the Wings of Men* in reference to the 1985 CHOGM:

> In 1985 . . . Pindling was a big thinker. (At CHOGM) (t) hey discussed Nelson Mandela in South Africa . . . dealing with how to get Mandela out of jail . . . to get others like Gandhi . . . Mulroney from Canada to confront Margaret Thatcher on this issue. We in the Commonwealth have to lead in getting Mandela out of Jail. The conclusions of that meeting changed politics in the US, in Europe and eventually lead to Mandela being freed.[16]

In respect to this great world leader who drove much of the discussion of CHOGM 1985 and champion for peace, I include this biographical sketch of Nelson Mandela:

---

16   http://www.thebahamasweekly.com/publish/arts-and- culture/Behind_the scenes on Bahamian documentary On the Wings of Men with_Franklin Wilson

Nelson Rolihlahla Mandela, born on July 18, 1918, in Transkei, South Africa, was the son of Hendry Mphakanyiswa. After his studies at University College of Fort Hare and the University of Witwatersrand, he obtained a law degree. Mandela's political career began in 1944, when he became a member of the African National Congress (ANC), where he joined in opposition to the apartheid regime in South Africa. He was tried for treason between 1956 and 1961 and was acquitted in1961.

Mandela is credited for establishing a militant wing of the ANC called the Umkhonto we Sizwe in the early 1960s. On June 12, 1964, eight members of the ANC, including Mandela were sentenced to life in prison for plotting to overthrow the South African government. He remained in prison from 1964 until his release in 1990. While in prison Mandela became an iconic hero of black resistance to oppressive white leadership in Africa and around the world.[17]

During his trial on April 20, 1964, Mandela uttered these now-famous words: "During my lifetime I have dedicated myself to this struggle of the African people . . . I have cherished the ideal of a democratic and free society in which all persons live together in harmony and with equal opportunities. It is an ideal which I hope to live for and to achieve. But if needs be, it is an ideal for which I am prepared to die."[18]

As a result of pressure from the international community, one such body being the commonwealth countries at the Nassau Accord, Mandela was freed from prison on February 11, 1990. He became the president of the ANC in 1991 and the president of South Africa in 1994.[19]

As stated before, I was not the only one who understood the significance of presenting to the world an intact government led by a credible leader who had the support of his people. Such a leader needed to be in place for a time such as this. The Commonwealth Heads of

17 http://www.nobelprize.org/nobel prizes/peace/laureates/1993/mandela-bio.html

18 www.goodreads.com/quotes/22390-during-my-lifetime-I-have-dedicatedmyself-to-this-struggle

19 http://www.nobelprize.org/nobel prizes/peace/laureates/1993/mandela-bio.html

Government had a tough battle to fight in its quest to bring down the apartheid regime in South Africa and some of the greatest resistance to plans put forward came from the Iron Lady herself. In full battle gear, here is how Sir Lynden addressed the gathering in his opening speech "Apartheid: An Abhorrent Policy":

> When we last met in New Delhi the question of South Africa and its abhorrent policy of apartheid featured prominently in our discussions. Two years later, South Africa has become more intransigent in its policies, more defiant of the United Nations Resolution calling for the independence of Namibia and openly aggressive in its violation of the territorial integrity of neighbouring countries like Lesotho and Botswana. Fortunately, in the words of U.S. Senator Edward Kennedy, "The sands of apartheid are running through the hour glass of international condemnation. The irresistible force of justice must one day prevail over the immovable object of apartheid."

> Friends and colleagues, I welcome you again to Nassau, one of the 700 beautiful spots in an archipelago of seven hundred beautiful islands.[20]

The *Tribune*[21] quotes Sir Lynden in his welcome address to the Commonwealth heads in the Rhythm Theatre, Cable Beach Casino appealing, "To sound a 'mighty crescendo' for negotiation in the present crisis in South Africa. Failing that, those who seek to make a peaceful solution impossible, may have in the process made a violent revolution inevitable."

Coming out of this historic occasion was the twenty-five-page Nassau Communiqué, presented by Sir Lynden and His Excellency Mr. Shridath Ramphal, Commonwealth secretary-general. This communiqué included the Commonwealth Accord on Southern Africa.

---

20   Excerpt from remarks made by Bahamas prime minister, the Rt. Hon. Sir Lynden Pindling, chairman, CHOGM '85 at the opening session.

21   October 16, 1985, edition of the *Tribune*

On the day before, October 21, the outlook was not as optimistic. Here is what Nicholas Ashford, on October 21, 1985, had to say:

> Mrs. Margaret Thatcher has maintained her solitary stand against economic sanctions against South Africa throughout a weekend of intense diplomatic activity, as Commonwealth leaders sought to reach agreement on a programme of joint action to end apartheid in the white-ruled republic. So far all attempts by a group of four Commonwealth leaders, who have been carrying out the negotiations with Mrs. Thatcher on behalf of the other 40-odd members of the association to persuade her to modify her implacable opposition to economic sanctions, have failed.[22]

The next day, on October 22, 1985, the horizon was clearer:

> Commonwealth leaders were yesterday congratulating themselves on reaching agreement on a package of measures increasing pressure on South Africa to end apartheid. But there were many differing interpretations on the extent to which Mrs. Margaret Thatcher had had to compromise to make agreement possible; the likely impact the accord would have on the South African Government; and what the fine print of the agreed seven-page document will actually entail.[23]

> According to the report,[24] Mrs. Thatcher was of the view that the other Commonwealth heads had fallen in line with her more moderate views on sanctions against South Africa in coming to an agreement. It asserts that Mrs. Thatcher, in fact, capitulated to the demands of her colleagues who were elated over the outcome of the negotiations. Ashford quoted President Kaunda of Zambia as saying that "This is a moment of great joy."

---

22 http://www.margaretthatcher.org/document/111649.

23 http://www.margaretthatcher.org/document/111649.

24 Ibid.

This moment of great joy was reached after a long and grueling weekend of negotiations between the Commonwealth heads. Much of it was spent being at odds with the Iron Lady, but in the end, Mrs. Thatcher admitted that "It was worth paying a price to get an agreement, it was worth paying a price to keep the Commonwealth together."[25]

In an effort to push for reform in South Africa, the accord sought to, by way of various sanctions, push for dialogue between black South African leaders and the government in Pretoria in an effort to dismantle apartheid.[26]

The accord outlined five steps toward the achievement of this goal. They included

1. the lifting of the state of emergency in South Africa;

2. the release of political prisoners, the chief among them being Nelson Mandela;

3. the lifting of the ban on the ANC;

4. the setting up of a committee to promote dialogue between black leaders and the white regime; and

5. the ceasing of all violence in the country on the part of all parties.

Further, the accord outlined nine sanctions that would be put in place against South Africa if it did not acquiesce to the demands. These included restrictions on the import of the Krugerrand and a ban on all new government loans to South Africa.[27]

I too, like Mrs. Thatcher in her capitulation, maintain that my not delivering the letter and the fallout that I received was worth paying the price for seeing Sir Lynden take his place as host of the 1985 CHOGM with his head held high. He did not have to enter the situation with the stain of being condemned in the form of a letter delivered by the president of the leading voice of the national conscience of the Bahamas, the Bahamas Christian Council.

Calvin Harris, producer of the film *Pindling: On the Wings of Men* has this to say in his synopsis of the film:

25   http://www.margaretthatcher.org/document/111649.

26   Ibid.

27   http://www.margaretthatcher.org/document/111649.

He faced two major hurdles in the 1980's. First (among them was), his decision, along with then Canadian Prime Minister Brian Mulroney, to push the political process forward which lead to the release of prisoner Nelson Mandela, who eventually became President of South Africa. To show his appreciation, Nelson Mandela's first flight from prison was to the Bahamas, to personally thank his good friend, a fellow student at the University of London in the 1950's, Sir Lynden Oscar Pindling.[28]

This must have been the reason why I did not sign or deliver the letter.

Our former prime minister, the right Honorable Hubert Ingraham, also weighs in on the significant role that Sir Lynden played in that historic 1985 CHOGM:

> The Bahamas has and continues to play its part in the affairs of the Commonwealth and remains committed to the principles of the organization. Indeed, The Bahamas was privileged to play a pivotal role in the dismantling of Apartheid in South Africa by extending the economic sanctions against the white minority government at the 1985 Commonwealth Heads of Government Meeting in Nassau.

> In fact, our former Prime Minister, the late Sir Lynden Oscar Pindling, was appointed Chairman of a group of Commonwealth Heads of Government to review the progress of the sanctions that eventually led to freeing from prison of Nelson Mandela and the peaceful transition to majority rule in South Africa.[29]

This must have been the reason why I did not sign or deliver the letter.

I have, over the years, firmly come to believe that my not having delivered that letter may have served to stay the cords of discontent which, if unleashed, would have served to hamper the creation and signing of what

---

28   http://www.thebahamasweekly.com/publish/bahamas-international-filmfestival/On the Wings of Men wins printer.shtml.

29   http://www.commonwealth-of-nations.org/Bahamas%6

is now the famous Nassau Accord, which called for the freeing of Nelson Mandela, the dismantling of the apartheid system, which established civil rights for black South Africans, and bringing to an end South Africa's occupation of Namibia.

CHAPTER 10

Looking Back

S IR LYNDEN COULD not be beaten at the poles, so they chose one man to do it, Philip Rahming, but he did not acquiesce to the plan. Locally, people were saying "Let's see what Lenny boy would do." Being "Lenny boy" was a debit as "Lenny boy" was from Fox Hill, and the saying was that no good thing could come out of Fox Hill. I was considered to be a natural spoiler, but that sentiment encouraged me to stand strong, and I did nothing. In this case, however, doing nothing was inaction, and inaction at this time was a powerful action that enabled the natural flow of the governmental process to unfold. The prime minister remained in charge and was able to chair the historic CHOGM 1985 in a country at peace. "Lenny boy" refused to deliver.

Rosa Parks refused to get up in that Montgomery bus, and this eventually led to the granting of civil rights in her country. It has been opined that if she had gone to the back of the bus, it would have taken the blacks backward. I refused to sign and deliver the letter, which I believe served to maintain civil order in my new, democratic, sovereign, and developing nation. This worked out in some way, through the accord that came out of CHOGM, which became the basis of civil rights in South Africa and eventually led to the release of Nelson Mandela from prison.

A black man led the Bahamas. It was a small country near a giant to the north, and this small country was doing well with black leadership, which began in 1967 following the historic majority rule victory of January 10. I had to think deeply on whether I would, in any way, either directly or indirectly, contribute to the pulling down of my country. I, especially being a Fox Hillian, did not want to have it said that black leadership failed. At the same time, I realized that others who were so determined to have the letter "go all the way" might have seen things differently.

Some persons are of the opinion that order can be created out of chaos, but the chaos that would have been created, had the letter been delivered, could not justify any ensuing order.

While there were those within ready to establish a utopia out of the ensuing chaos, there were other more powerful forces waiting on the outside, ready to take the leader out if they felt it was warranted, as was the case in the Philippines with Marcos. In my opinion the "fever" that ensues from external interference always takes a longer time to dissipate than change brought about from within. Naomi Klein, in her book *The Shock Doctrine*, has dubbed this phenomenon of external interference "disaster capitalism." It occurs when certain adventurers deliberately instigate upheaval within a nation and then proceed to move in under the guise of bringing about the order they desire, but first, they wait for one of its own dearly beloved sons to begin the destruction.

Mandela was released at a time when the world was in need of powerful leaders. In stature and form, he was an imposing figure, yet he was humble. He did not step off Robin Island with a boxer's stance but came out of his corner filled with calm humility and a willingness to lead and reconcile. He stood as a lion for attention but as a lamb for service. Herein lies the paradox. This is what happened, and in retrospect, I am able to stand firm and contend that this is why I could not and did not deliver the letter. Today we still have a beautiful, continuing, developing, democratic, and sovereign nation.

We were a new nation situated within the waters of the Atlantic Ocean. Our nation was the place to which Ponce de Leon traveled to find the fountain of youth. Our nation, the Bahamas, became the place where CHOGM heralded the rebirth stimulus for Nelson Mandela and South Africa. What Ponce de Leon did not find, Nelson Mandela found in a rejuvenation to lead the country that once imprisoned him. All this came about as a result of the work done by Sir Lynden and the other eminent leaders at CHOGM '85.

This is why I could not and did not deliver the letter.

Today, fifty years after majority rule, we still have a beautiful, continuing developing country led by the Honorable Dr. Hubert Minnis, prime minister, as a result of the work done by Sir Lynden Oscar Pindling of the Bahamas and other distinguished and eminent leaders of CHOGM '85. When good works are left alone to grow and blossom, we can see the fruits they bear. This, in part, came to pass because of this unsigned and undelivered letter, because I remained strong, listened, and obeyed the inner voice. Our Bahamas stands a vibrant, free nation, and the journey continues. The late Nelson R. Mandela, a champion for liberation and democracy, was set free, and we in the Bahamas have done our part; and we remain as stated by our pledge, one people united in love and service.

CHAPTER II

The Unsigned Letter

THE BAHAMAS CHRISTIAN COUNCIL

P.O. BOX SS 5863

NASSAU*COMMONWEALTH OF THE BAHAMAS

18th March, 1985

PRESIDENT
Rev. Dr. Philip Rahming, J.P.
Telephone: 3-6550, 3-4808
P.O. Box 5304

VICE-PRESIDENT
Rev. Albert H. Hepburn
Telephone: 9-4009/2 8700

SECRETARY
Fr. Kirkley C. Sands
Telephone: 3-219?

ASSISTANT SECRETARY
Rev. William L. Beard
Telephone: 3-2534

TREASURER
Pastor Richard Bancs
Telephone: 9-8700

The Hon. Sir Lynden O. Pindling
Prime Minister,
Of The Commonwealth of
The Bahamas,
Nassau, Bahamas.

<u>BY HAND:</u>

Dear Mr. Prime Minister,

Greetings in the Name of Our Lord Jesus Christ, the
Head of the Church who has commanded us to preach
the Gospel to all Nations, teaching them to observe
all things whatsoever he has commanded us.

Sir, the Leaders of the member Churches of The
Bahamas Christian Council, together with some who
hold Observer Status in that body, have given careful
and prayerful consideration to certain allegations
brought against our Prime Minister in recent months.

The testimonies given by yourself and others before
the Commission of Inquiry have left you and your high
office in an apparent compromising position which
embarrasses and concerns us.

We hold the office of Prime Minister in high esteem
and in our view this office should exemplify
something of the quality of leadership spoken of by
Our Lord when he said, "But whosoever will be great
among you shall be your minister, and whosoever of
you will be the chiefest shall be servant of all."
(Mark 10:42-43) - K.J.V.

We believe it our duty, as Leaders of the Christian
Churches in The Bahamas, to let you know that we
find your acceptance of certain gifts from sources,
known and unknown, morally questionable.

If we keep silent, we might seem to be party, if
not to your actions, to any future actions of those
who use their position in society to receive gifts
and favours. Also, we may seem to be agreeing to a

EXECUTIVE COUNCIL MEMBERS
Canon William B. Thompson
Telephone: 3-2940

Bishop Harcourt Pinder
Telephone: 3-2710

Rev. Mrs. Ruth C. Bastian
Telephone: 5-0745

Rev. Donald Sands
Telephone: 3-1735

EX OFFICIO MEMBERS
Heads of Churches

EX OFFICIO VICE-PRESIDENTS
a. Grand Bahama Branch
b. North Andros Branch

-2-

The Hon. Sir Lynden O. Pindling   18th March,1985

precedent for future leaders of our young Nation
to follow. We would like to uphold the principle
that people who serve in Public Offices should
never act, nor appear to act, under the pressure
of having received gifts.

You have a fine record of leadership and service
to our beloved Bahamas. This is now being
questioned, we therefore urge you to pray for
guidance and seek, as a humble servant of God and
of our people, an early solution to this problem.
We are prepared to discuss, with you, the matter
at hand, with a view to finding a righteous solution.

                              Yours faithfully,

                              The Rev. Dr. Philip Rahming
                              President
                              The Bahamas Christian Council.

BIBLIOGRAPHY

1. www.washingtonpost.com

2. Taken from "The Letter" dated March 18, 1985, from The Bahamas Christian Council to Sir Lynden.

3. Taken from "The Letter" dated March 18, 1985, from The Bahamas Christian Council to Sir Lynden.

4. Information contained in a letter from Pastor Roach to Doctor Rahming.

5. "The Vision of Sir Lynden Pindling: In His Own Words: Letters and Speeches, 1948–1997."

6. Printed with permission of Bishop Delton D. Fernander, President Bahamas Christian Council.

7. https://books.google.bs/books?id=UYGDFHov1b8C&pg=PA212&lpg=%20PA212&dq=the+jesuit+order+reached+the+pinnacle+of+its+power%20&source%20=%20bl&ots%20=%20i1ACBLGX3e&sig%20=%20b%20WQ0JcjKk4IUDGrgYawu%20Sp1oJc&hl=en&sa=X&ved=%200ahUKEwiCy4KPnf%20LVAhVBQiYKHYj%20CVIQ6AEIJjAA#v=onepage&q=the%20jesuit%20order%20reached%%2020the%20pinnacle%20of%20its%20power&f=false.

8. https://www.scribd.com/doc/30408550/Quotes-About-the-Jesuit-Order- From-Famous-People.

9. https://www.bl.uk/collection-items/the-trial-of-henry-garnet-1606.

10. http://www.thebahamasweekly.com/publish/arts-and-culture/Behind the scenes on Bahamian documentary On the Wings of Men with Franklin Wils on.

11. http://www.nobelprize.org/nobel prizes/peace/laureates/1993/mandela- bio.html.

12. www.goodreads.com/quotes/22390-during-my-lifetime-I-have-dedicated- myself-to-this—struggle.

13. Excerpt from remarks made by Bahamas Prime Minister, the Rt. Hon. Sir Lynden Pindling, Chairman, CHOGM – '85 at the Opening Session.

14. October16, 1985 edition of The Tribune.

15. http://www.margaretthatcher.org/document/111649

16. http://www.thebahamasweekly.com/publish/bahamas-international-film—festival/On the Wings of Men wins printer.shtml

17. http://www.commonwealth-of-nations.org/Bahamas%6